IMAGES

HISTORIC NORTH SYDNEY

RANNIE GILLIS

NIMBUS PUBLISHING

Nimbus Publishing Limited
PO Box 9166
Halifax, NS B3K 5M8
(902) 455-4286

Printed and bound in Canada
Design: Terri Strickland

Printed and bound in Canada

Title page: North Sydney, 1882—A wonderful old wood engraving from the book *Picturesque Canada*, published in Toronto in 1882 by the Royal Canadian Academy of Arts. Sketched from the top of Goat Hill, or Chapel Hill as it was then known, this view to the south gives a panoramic view of the rapidly expanding town. In the foreground is the town's first Roman Catholic church (1844), while the massive coal shipping piers (1834) are visible in the lower left. Also prominent is the "weather mast," a signal station on the top of Goat Hill where coloured flags would indicate weather conditions or approaching storms for the benefit of ships in the harbour.

Library and Archives Canada Cataloguing in Publication

Gillis, Rannie.
Historic North Sydney / Rannie Gillis
Includes bibliographical references.
ISBN 1551095408

1. North Sydney (N.S.)—History–Pictorial works. I. Title.

FC2349.N6G54 2005   71.6'95 22   C2005906028X

Canada

The Canada Council for the Arts | Le Conseil des Arts du Canada

We acknowledge the financial support of the Government of Canada through the Book Publishing Industry Development Program (BPIDP) and the Canada Council, and of the Province of Nova Scotia through the Department of Tourism, Culture and Heritage for our publishing activities.

This book is dedicated to my sister, Catherine Anne Gillis, and to Maria.

Acknowledgements

This book would not have been possible without the help and encouragement of the following individuals, who gave freely of their time and expertise in providing photographs, archival research material, computers and scanners, and valuable insights and knowledge into the history of North Sydney and surrounding area.

The staff at the North Sydney Historical Society: Jim Walsh, president; Albert Wilkie, treasurer; Ron MacDonald, secretary; Tom Rose, researcher; Craig Organ, information technologist.

The staff of the Beaton Institute at Cape Breton University: Wendy Robicheau, director; Anne MacLean, archival researcher; Anne Connell, archival clerk; Donelda MacDonald, archival clerk; April MacLean, student researcher.

Special thanks to: Gary Gallivan, for unlimited access to the more than two thousand Cape Breton images in his private collection; Art Rice, for permission to access the many fine photographs taken by his father Nelson Rice; Neil Libbey; for his knowledge and help in researching archival photos; Kristy Read, a graphic arts graduate of Cape Breton University who scanned and retouched all the images in this book.

The following individuals provided one or more archival photos: Arlene MacDonald; Stan Jesty; Jim Cogan; Robert Shebib; Marty Andrea (Branch 19-Royal Canadian Legion); Frank McNamara (St. Joseph's Parish).

Special mention should also be made of the two invaluable, extensively-researched books by North Sydney native Elva Jackson: *Cape Breton and the Jackson Kith and Kin* and *Windows on the Past,* both of which contain a wealth of information on North Sydney's history and inhabitants.

Finally, a very special thank you to Ann Marie MacLean, whose special interest and encouragement kept me going during those extended periods of research and manuscript preparation.

Contents

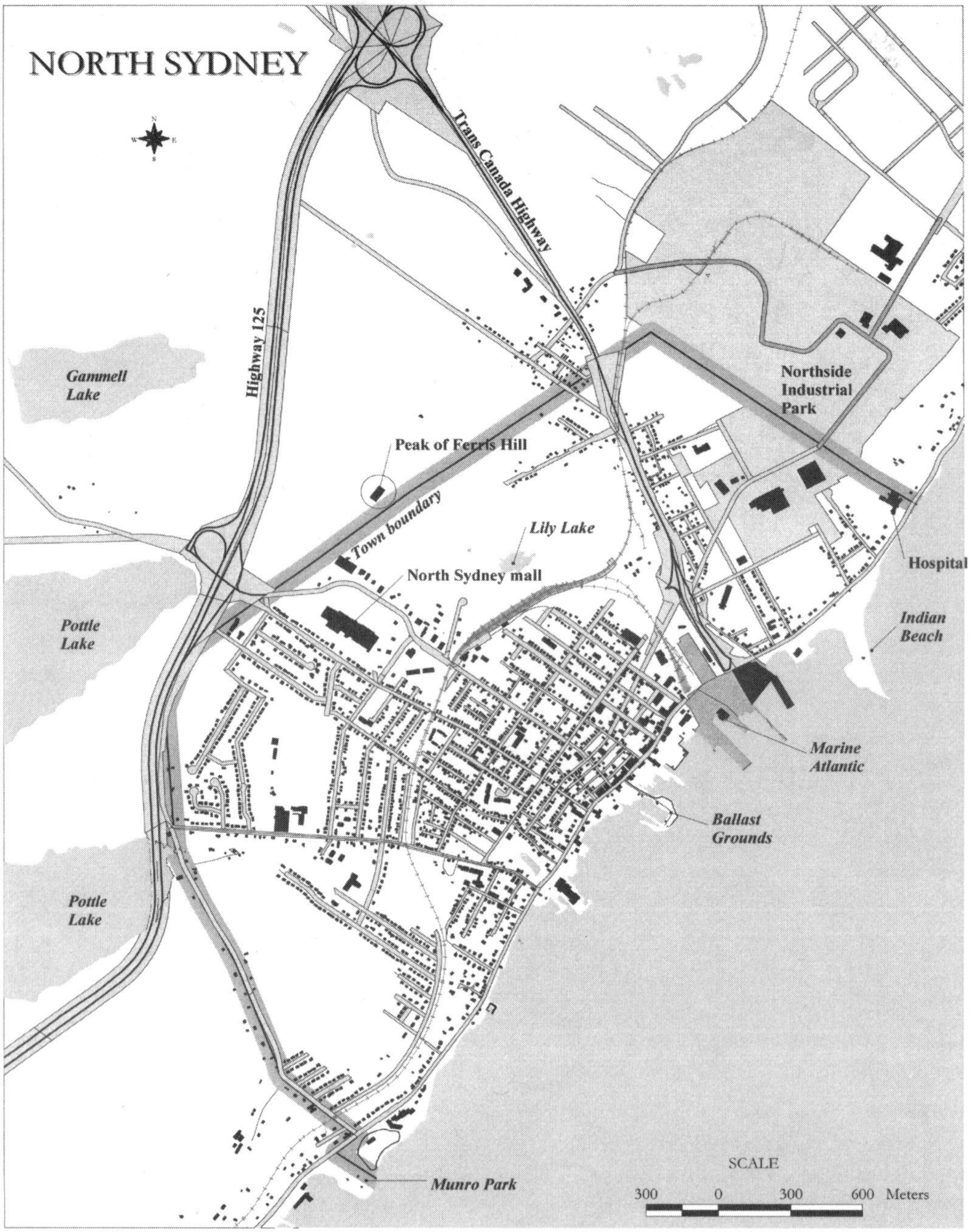

North Sydney's Population

These statistics are from the National Census, held every ten years in Canada since 1871.

Year	North Sydney	CBRM*
1891	2,522	34,244
1911	5,418	73,330
1941	6,838	110,703
1961	8,657	131,507
2001	6,775	109,330

*The CBRM (Cape Breton Regional Municipality) includes Sydney, North Sydney, Sydney Mines, New Waterford, Dominion, Glace Bay, Louisbourg, and the rest of Cape Breton County. The CBRM came into existence on August 1, 1995, through the amalgamation of these eight municipalities. The CBRM is the second largest municipality in Nova Scotia, with an area of 2,470 square kilometres.

Introduction

What's in a name? Quite a bit, it seems, especially if you are referring to North Sydney! Already ranked as the fourth largest seaport (by traffic volume) in the Dominion of Canada in the 1870s, in that decade the little town became known as "Canada's Gateway to Europe" with the arrival of the Western Union underwater telegraph cable from Ireland. Since 1898, when the first scheduled Newfoundland ferry arrived in North Sydney, our safe anchorage has also been known as the "Gateway to Newfoundland."

As far back as the early 1800s, this snug little fishing port on the "north-side" of Sydney Harbour was also known as the "Bar Town." Whether this name was complimentary or derogatory depends on which of two conflicting anecdotes you believe. The first states that the village received its name because of the large sand bar in the area. This natural breakwater made—and still makes—it possible for ships to drop anchor safely in the calm waters of the inner harbour. The second explanation claims that the name was bestowed in honour of the many taverns, or bars, that dotted the waterfront.

Mi'kmaq Camp, Bras D'Or Lakes, c.1820

This anonymous portrait from about 1820 gives a vivid illustration of a typical Mi'kmaq camp that would have been found on the shores of the Bras D'Or Lakes. Fish and wildfowl were staples of the Mi'kmaq diet, and along with the meat of various animals provided a healthy source of nourishment.

Considering that Sydney Harbour was one of the busiest fishing ports in the Maritime Provinces, the latter might not be such a far-fetched idea.

Be that as it may, the more serious (and sober) local inhabitants decided that the "Bar Town" was not a suitable name for their rapidly growing community. Subsequently, on March 29, 1841, the good members of the Nova Scotia Legislature in Halifax passed an act stating that the tiny community on the "north-side" of Sydney Harbour would henceforth be known as "The Township of North Sydney."

First Settlers

The first permanent settlers on the north shore of Sydney Harbour were aboriginals, members of the Mi'kmaq First Nation who arrived in Cape Breton Island around ten thousand years ago, shortly after the end of the last great ice age. They built seasonal encampments on the local sand bar (today's Indian Beach), and a permanent camp behind the present town, on the side of Ferris Hill. In accordance with the Centralization Policy of 1942, the Mi'kmaq inhabitants of North Sydney were forcibly removed by the federal government in a misguided attempt to mitigate the social and economic effects of the Great Depression on the Mi'kmaq population of Nova Scotia. Families and individuals from twenty locations were relocated to one of two reserves: Eskasoni, for those living on Cape Breton Island, and Shubenacadie, for those on the mainland of Nova Scotia. Needless to say, the policy was a resounding failure, and led to the many intractable problems faced by today's Mi'kmaq population.

The first people of European descent who visited the area were undoubtedly the Norsemen, or Vikings, probably around 1000 A.D. Recent research has also indicated that Basque fishermen from France and Spain could have visited the Grand Banks of Newfoundland and the shores of Cape Breton Island well before the voyages of Christopher Columbus and John Cabot.

However, while the identity of the first European visitors may always remain uncertain, the names of the first two men of European descent who settled on the north-side of Sydney harbour are known. Adam Moore and Duncan Campbell, originally from Scotland, were United Empire Loyalists from the eastern United States who came to Cape Breton in 1784, following the American Revolution. After spending the winter months in Louisbourg, Moore and Campbell arrived in Sydney in the spring of 1785 and received land grants in what is now called upper North Sydney. They were soon joined by several other Loyalist families, such as the Allens, Jacksons, Moffats, and Musgraves. Many descendants from these families can still be found within the town boundaries—some have even remained on the original land grants.

Growing Business and Industry

By the early 1800s, North Sydney was one of the busiest fishing ports in eastern Canada, with vessels calling from all parts of the Maritimes and the eastern United States. It expanded even more after 1834, when the General

NORTH SYDNEY & BRAS D'OR LAKES, C.1940

A lovely aerial photo of the town with the Bras D'Or Lakes in the upper background. The seven-mile-long Pottle's Lake, which provides the water supply for the entire north-side, occupies most of the centre image, while Cranberry Lake is visible centre right. The smaller body of water below these, on the right side, is Lily Lake, at the station end of Blowers Street. North Bar (Indian Beach), with its offshore sandbar just visible, is at the lower right. The long, black wharf just above it is the old coal-shipping pier, in use between 1902 and 1964. The longest wharf is the Newfoundland Ferry Terminal, while the "U"-shaped ballast grounds to its left were not physically connected to the town's waterfront at the time the picture was taken. The large cleared area in the lower right above Indian Beach is the quarry where rock and fill were excavated for the construction of the new Newfoundland Terminus Wharf which opened in 1958.

Mining Association built a large pier for shipping coal from neighbouring Sydney Mines, which did not have a protected harbour from which to ship it to market. A few early attempts had been made to build coal piers at Lloyd's Cove and Sutherland's Corner, but these did not last very long, due to the combined effects of northeast gales and seasonal pack ice.

In 1834 a three-mile long railroad was completed from the pithead in Sydney Mines to the new coal pier in North Sydney. This was one of the first railroads in North America to be built with iron rails (from England), and one of the first to use the standard gauge of 4 feet 8½ inches. A unique system was devised for hauling the coal. For approximately half the distance, horses pulled the coal cars up a slight grade to the top of Goat Hill. At the top of the grade, the horses were unharnessed, placed in an empty car at the rear, and the coal train was allowed to glide down to the pier. To return to the pithead, the process was reversed. The hard-working horses were replaced with small locomotives in 1854.

As there was no coal in Newfoundland and Prince Edward Island, a thriving coal export business soon developed in North Sydney. Large ships carried coal to larger centres like St. John's and Summerside, while smaller vessels and schooners delivered coal to coastal villages and outport communities. Each year the coal shipments grew by a significant margin. Fortunately, major changes in transport technology were just around the corner.

The invention of the steam engine, for both commercial and military use, brought about a revolution in ocean transport and led to a rapid expansion of North Sydney's marine supply services. The first early steamships still carried sails, but as the technology developed, sails became redundant, and steam power ruled the waves. Suddenly North Sydney was no longer just a fishing port, or a place to export coal—now it became a mandatory stopover for commercial shipping traffic and the navies of the world.

By the early 1850s, steamships from Canada and the United States were stopping at North Sydney to take on coal before setting out on the two-thousand-mile journey across the North Atlantic. Ships arriving in Canada from Europe also stopped to replenish their coal supplies before continuing on to their destinations. As well, steam-powered warships from the British Royal Navy, the French Navy, and the United States Navy called at North Sydney to fill up their coal bunkers before setting out on patrol in the North Atlantic or along the eastern seaboard of North America.

By 1875 North Sydney had become the fourth largest seaport in Canada in terms of tonnage handled, exceeded only by Quebec City, Halifax, and Montreal. That same year also saw the opening of the Western Union Cable Office in North Sydney. The town thus became the terminus for all undersea telegraph messages between North America and Europe.

Only twenty-three years later, in 1892, the Intercolonial Railroad from central Canada finally reached the town. Soon after that, British and Canadian politicians decided that North Sydney would be the mainland terminus for a proposed ferry service between the Dominions of Canada and Newfoundland. Early on the morning of July 1, 1898, the SS *Bruce* arrived in North Sydney from Port aux Basques. Its arrival marked the inauguration of regular scheduled passenger and freight service between the two Dominions.

But first, it is important not to underestimate the importance of the trans-Atlantic cable to North Sydney. Back in 1858, when the first successful underwater telegraph cable between North America and Europe was successfully laid, it was the scientific equivalent of putting a man on the moon. The original cable station at this end was in Aspy Bay, in northern Cape Breton. The telegraph signal went from Aspy Bay to Port aux Basques, then on to Hearts Content, on the east coast of Newfoundland. From there it went under the ocean, at an average depth of twelve thousand feet, to Valentia Island in

Ireland. From Valentia it was sent under the Irish Sea to England. It took more than thirty minutes to transmit the first messages across the North Atlantic. Even so, such timing was infinitely better than the four to six weeks it took to send a message across the Atlantic Ocean by ship. However, the new cable broke within a few months, and could not be repaired. In spite of several attempts, it would take another eight years before a new, improved, cable was put in place.

In 1875, the Cape Breton end of the cable was transferred from Aspy Bay to the north side of Sydney Harbour, and a new cable office was built in North Sydney. This move was nescessary because severe pack ice conditions each spring played havoc with the underwater cable.This little town then became the "Canadian connection" for all undersea telegraph messages between North America and Europe. North Sydney was now known as "Canada's Gateway to the (European) World."

When it first opened, the new cable office had a staff of twenty-five operators. By 1900, there were between fifty and sixty operators, and they had to move to a larger building. The volume of telegrams increased to the point where it was not unusual for more than four thousand messages to be transmitted during an eight-hour shift!

By 1913, the total number of messages transmitted during an eight-hour shift had increased to over ten thousand, and the company decided to build a new and much larger office building. They purchased land at the upper end of Court Street and construction started immediately. The official opening of the new "Cable Office," the largest in North America, took place in December, 1914.

Two historic incidents, in less than three years, further thrust North Sydney into the international spotlight. The first event took place on the night of April 15, 1912, when the local cable office relayed the news that the world's largest and supposedly "unsinkable" passenger ship had struck an iceberg and was sinking off the coast of Newfoundland. When the *Titanic* sank later that night, along with more than fifteen hundred passengers and crew, North Sydney became a focal point for frantic telegrams from both sides of the Atlantic Ocean. News organizations worldwide wanted immediate access to casualty lists and other pertinent information related to this unprecedented disaster.

Little more than two years later, in August 1914, the outbreak of World War One resulted in the North Sydney cable office being placed on a full "war footing." For the next four years, armed soldiers patrolled its grounds, public access was greatly restricted, and certain hand-picked telegraphers received special training in sending and receiving secretly-coded military messages. By the end of the war in 1918, the cable office had a civilian and military staff of more than three hundred.

Although World War One officially came to an end at 11 A.M., November 11, 1918, the residents of North Sydney and surrounding towns celebrated this momentous news a day earlier. It seems that a certain telegrapher had told his wife of a top-secret message he had decoded earlier that morning—something to the effect that news of the end of the war would be released to the general public the next morning, on the eleventh. Needless to say, by the early afternoon of November 10, the news was out. Schools and businesses closed early, the liquor stores gave away their supplies, huge bonfires were lit, and people on both sides of Sydney Harbour celebrated the end of the "War To End All Wars." The rest of the world had to wait until the next day!

During World War Two (1939–1945) the North Sydney cable office was once again a beehive of activity, although not quite as hectic as during the first war. By this time there were many different cables running under the Atlantic Ocean, and the military and civilian traffic could be handled in a more organized manner. Inevitably, however, unusual things did happen, such as the game of trans-Atlantic chess (in secret code) played between British Prime Minister Winston Churchill and American President Franklin Roosevelt. Local telegraphers set up a chess board so that they could follow the progress of the game! After the war, advances in technology and equipment led to a fairly rapid decrease in the number of telegraphers and operators required. By 1962, the Western Union cable office in North Sydney closed its doors, and the few remaining men were transferred to company headquarters in New York City. A significant chapter in the town's history had come to an end.

Newfoundland Ferry Service

Although the Intercolonial Railway from Central Canada reached North Sydney by 1892, it was not until 1897 that the town was designated as the Canadian terminus for the proposed ferry service to Newfoundland. This decision involved much discussion between the town officials, British and Canadian politicians, and the owners of the Reid Newfoundland Railway. As well, the local mayor and town council had to fight off a determined effort by politicians and business leaders in Sydney, who wanted the ferry terminus for their side of the harbour.

However, the decision was made, and early in the morning of July 1, 1898, the SS *Bruce* sailed into the harbour at North Sydney. The two British Dominions in North America, Canada and Newfoundland, were now linked by a scheduled ferry service that would provide three round-trip crossings every week.

For the next thirteen years the *Bruce* carried more than three hundred thousand passengers back and forth across the often turbulent waters of the Cabot Strait. When Sydney Harbour was closed due to the spring pack ice, the *Bruce* would sail into Louisbourg Harbour, from where the passengers made their way to North Sydney by train.

Then, on March 24, 1911, the *Bruce* ran aground on a rocky ledge between Scatarie Island and Louisbourg. In spite of the best efforts of the crew, two of the 123 passengers were lost, and the ship quickly broke apart on the hidden reef. The first chapter in the Newfoundland ferry service had come to a tragic end.

While a replacement vessel was under construction in Scotland, two smaller ships from the Newfoundland coastal service took over the task of providing ferry service across the Cabot Strait. Less than two years later, the new ice-reinforced ship, also named the *Bruce*, arrived and continued to operate on the regular service until 1915. It was then sold to the Russian government for use as an icebreaker.

When the *Bruce* left, the SS *Kyle* was transferred from the Labrador service to operate on the Cabot Strait. Built in Scotland in 1913, its hull had also been reinforced to operate in heavy ice conditions, and it easily fitted into its new role. For the next ten years the *Kyle* offered steady, dependable service between Nova Scotia and Newfoundland, even in severe spring ice conditions.

By the time the *Kyle* arrived in 1915, World War One had been raging for more than a year. Now, on both sides of the Cabot Strait, the Canadian and British military had a crucial role to play in the operation of the Newfoundland ferry service. For the duration of the war, the *Kyle* continued to move surreptitiously between the two ports, changing its route on a regular basis and usually sailing without military escort. It survived the war unscathed. It was also at this time that the first coastal defence installations were built in Sydney and Port aux Basques harbours.

In 1925, a brand new ship arrived to take over the Cabot Strait service. The SS *Caribou*, built in Holland, represented a new level of luxury and convenience for the Newfoundland ferry service. Over the next seventeen years the *Caribou* set a new standard for reliability and on-time performance, and its ice-reinforced hull enabled it to keep on schedule except in the worst possible ice conditions.

With the outbreak of World War Two in 1939, the Newfoundland ferry service once again went on a wartime footing. The *Caribou* continued to slip in and out of North Sydney and Port aux Basques in the middle of the night, unannounced, and without following a regular route or schedule. It always travelled without visible lights and usually without a destroyer or naval corvette to act as escort.

The *Caribou*'s luck held until the night of October 14, 1942. At 3:20 A.M., two torpedoes from an enemy submarine slammed into its side, and the ship slipped beneath the waves in less than five minutes. Of the 238 passengers and crew, only 101 survived. Because of wartime security, it was three days before the sinking was officially confirmed. However, news travels fast in a seaport town, and the residents of both North Sydney and Port aux Basques were fully aware of the extent of the tragedy within a few hours.

With the loss of the *Caribou* the SS *Burgeo* was recalled from the Newfoundland coastal service and took over the dangerous journey for the final three years of the war. Like the *Caribou* before it, the ferry made three round trips a week, always at night, and usually without a military escort. Thanks to the courage and skill of its determined crew, it managed to survive the war.

With the end of the war in 1945, things slowly returned to normal for the ships of the Newfoundland ferry service. One of the first priorities was to replace the *Caribou*, and an order for a new ice-reinforced vessel was placed in Scotland. Two years later, on August 10, 1947, the SS *Cabot Strait* made its first voyage across the body of water after which it had been named. Full-time passenger and freight service had now been restored to the Newfoundland service. However, unknown to just about everyone, unforeseen revolutionary changes were about to change forever the nature and rationale of the Newfoundland ferry service.

On March 31, 1949, Newfoundland became the tenth province of Canada. Under the terms of union, the Canadian government assumed full responsibility for the Newfoundland transportation system. This included the Newfoundland Railway, the coastal ferry service, and the transportation link across the Cabot Strait. A new era was about to begin.

NORTH SYDNEY FROM SEVEN THOUSAND FEET. C.1962

This Department of National Defence photo, with sunlight reflecting off the harbour in the upper left, by Point Edward, gives an excellent overview of North Sydney and its surrounding areas. Pottle's Lake and Cranberry Lake dominate the right half of the picture, with Johnston's Road running in a perfectly straight line to Christie's Wharf at Little Bras D'Or.

The curved road behind Pottle's Lake is the "Old Branch Road", the original 1892 route of the Intercolonial Raliway from the junction at George's River to the new station in North Sydney. Closer inspection will reveal Lily Lake, behind the raliway station, and the circular water reservoir on the top of Ferris Street. The oval-shaped race track, at the Farmers' Exhibition Grounds off Regent Street, is in the middle of the picture.

Notice in the top right and centre the long, narrow, rectangular outlines of farms and other properties. These original land grants, which have not been broken up or sub-divided, extended from the harbour to Pottle's Lake, or from Pottle's Lake to the Bras D'Or Lakes.

North Sydney and the Military

North Sydney's historic role in both world wars extended to its role as a gathering spot for civilian and military vessels waiting to join convoys. It also served as the location of an important naval air station at Kelly's Beach (known by today's generation as Munro Park).

A military presence, of one sort or another, has been associated with Sydney Harbour for almost the last three hundred years, and North Sydney has always played a very active role in this aspect of the area's history. One of the first recorded defence installations in Canada was a small fort at the entrance to the harbour, built in 1741 by Colonel Armstrong, then Governor of Cape Breton Island. One year later a small naval battle took place just outside the harbour entrance, between French ships and privateers from the New England colonies.

Following the outbreak of World War One in 1914, a second fort with several gun emplacements was built on the same site where Armstrong's fort once stood, and other coastal defence installations were built on both sides of the harbour. The new overseas conflict required large amounts of military and civilian supplies, most of which came from Canada and the United States. By 1917, German submarines were sinking so many supply ships that a convoy system was put in place in order to protect Allied shipping.

The main convoy assembly points in Canada were Halifax and Sydney–North Sydney. The defences of these two harbours were quickly upgraded to provide secure gathering places for civilian ships preparing to cross the Atlantic Ocean. (St. John's, Newfoundland, was primarily an assembly and refuelling point for naval escort vessels.)

A joint Canadian–American naval air station was also set up at Kelly's Beach, from which primitive seaplanes known as "flying boats" could provide anti-submarine air patrols for the convoys setting out on their dangerous journeys across the North Atlantic Ocean. These amphibious machines would land in the water and run up on floating cradles which would then be towed up on shore. The process was reversed when they wanted to take off.

The station had four Curtiss flying boats, each with a flying time of about five hours, and a patrol range of between seventy-five and one hundred miles. Not very far, especially when considering that the distance between Sydney Harbour and the west coast of England is approximately two thousand miles. So what was their purpose?

The flying boats actually had two roles to play. If all went according to plan, the convoys would be escorted all the way across the ocean by naval vessels from the Canadian, American, or British navies. With that in mind, the first role of the flying boats was to provide local, or "close to shore" support, for one of the most dangerous times for any convoy is just after it has left the safety of a well-defended harbour.

Each flying boat usually carried a single machine gun, a few small bombs, and a radio. Although not designed to actually attack an enemy submarine, its main purpose was to notify accompanying naval vessels if an enemy submarine was spotted on the ocean surface, or at a shallow depth underwater. The warships would then attempt to destroy the sub with deck guns or by ramming. If the enemy sub went under, they would then use depth charges.

The second, equally important role of the flying boat was purely psychological. The sight and sound of these flimsy flying machines was encouraging to the local population and, even more important, to the civilian crews of the many merchant ships that were forming up in Sydney and Halifax harbours. The fact that their single machine guns and tiny bombs would likely do little damage to an enemy submarine was beside the point. At least the government and military leaders could say that they were using every means at their disposal to protect the convoys.

By the end of the war in November, 1918, the facilities at Kelly's Beach could accommodate four hundred men, two hundred Canadian and two hundred American! Two large wooden barracks had been built on the side of the hill, along with a number of storage and warehouse buildings and a large seaplane hangar located just back from the beach. With the end of the war, all the buildings were boarded up, and the hangar was demolished.

Twenty years later, with the outbreak of World War Two (1939–1945), North Sydney once again found itself at the forefront of the Canadian war effort. This time, however, the convoy system was split into two distinct components. The "fast" convoys, containing ships which could maintain a speed of at least ten knots, sailed from Halifax. The "slow" convoys, with ships that travelled at a slower speed, left from Sydney–North Sydney. An interesting sidenote: because of intense lobbying and pressure from Sydney politicians, all ships carrying explosives were required to anchor in the Northwest Arm of the harbour, near Upper North Sydney!

With the outbreak of war, the military base at Kelly's Beach was quickly reactivated. A new seaplane hangar was built, and a squadron of flying boats soon arrived, able to provide anti-submarine cover for a distance of at least a thousand miles from shore. Once again, as in World War One, the sheer presence of these large, noisy aircraft provided a psychological and morale boost to both the local inhabitants and the thousands of sailors and merchant seamen waiting patiently aboard their cramped ships.

With the end of the war in 1945, the naval air station at Kelly's Beach was once again shut down. Buildings were boarded up, and in the early 1950s the large seaplane hangar was turned into a Vocational School. Finally, in 1959, the town was able to buy the land back from the Department of National Defence. Today, four of the original World War Two military buildings still exist: one on the harbour, and three on the side of the hill by Musgrave Lane.

While most of the military facilities at Kelly's Beach (Munro Park) are long gone, an interesting souvenir from World War One still sits at the North Sydney Museum, located in the bottom of the former Bank of Nova Scotia on Commercial Street. It is a six-foot-long wooden propeller, attached to a wall, which is all that remains from one of the American Curtiss Flying Boats that flew from Kelly's Beach in 1917!

North Sydney and the Future

Over the last half-century, North Sydney, like all industrial towns on Cape Breton Island, has seen its industrial base erode away. In the late 1950s, more than eleven hundred people worked at the Newfoundland ferry terminal. Of these, more than one thousand were stevedores, who handled the large amount of freight that moved back and forth between Nova Scotia and Newfoundland.

Most freight would arrive by rail and would have to be unloaded from the rail cars and loaded into the waiting boats. The rail cars could not be shipped directly to Port aux Basques because the railway in Newfoundland used a different railroad gauge, and Canadian rail cars would not fit on Newfoundland tracks. Everything had to be unloaded in North Sydney, shipped across the Cabot Strait, and loaded back into waiting trains in Port aux Basques. It was a labour-intensive process. Today, virtually all freight arrives by truck, and containerization has put an end to large numbers of stevedores working at their task. Today, less than thirty stevedores are employed, mainly to receive the lines and tie up the ferries when they arrive at the dock.

In 1955, six years after Newfoundland's entry into Confederation, the MV *William Carson* arrived in North Sydney. A revolutionary vessel, it was the first Canadian-built ship to operate in the Newfoundland service and the first designed to carry automobiles. (Before the *Carson,* cars and trucks had to be hoisted on board the Newfoundland ferry, and lashed down on top of the cargo holds!)

With the completion of the Newfoundland portion of the Trans-Canada Highway in 1965, the amount of vehicle traffic to Newfoundland doubled overnight. The MV *Patrick Morris,* a rail-car ferry which could carry forty box-cars of freight, was added to the Newfoundland service, and over the next twenty years several other ships were rented or purchased to help with the rapidly increasing volume of traffic to Newfoundland.

Finally, in 1986, the first of two brand new "superferries" arrived in North Sydney. The MV *Caribou* could carry twelve hundred passengers and up to 350 automobiles on two vehicle decks. Its sister ship, the MV *Joseph and Clara Smallwood,* arrived four years later. With each vessel capable of making two round-trip crossings a day, almost five thousand people, and fourteen hundred automobiles could be transported across the Cabot Strait in one twenty-four-hour period.

In 2002, a new record was set when 528,975 passengers were moved across the Cabot Strait. That same year more than 172,000 cars and 79,000 trucks were ferried across. As the rest of North America continues to discover the many attractions of Newfoundland and Labrador, these figures should continue to increase.

However, although more than half-a-million people passed through North Sydney in 2002, very few of these travellers made any effort to spend any amount of time, or money, in the little seaport town. Trying to entice some of these people to visit North Sydney remains an ongoing problem that has so far defied a reasonable solution.

In the early 1980s, with help from provincial and federal governments, an industrial park was set up on Goat Hill. Located between North Sydney and

Sydney Mines, the new park was expected to lead to a renaissance in industrial activity on the north side of Sydney Harbour. Unfortunately, like most projects of this kind, the eagerly anticipated industries failed to materialize. Today, twenty years later, more than three hundred good-paying jobs do exist in the Northside Industrial Park. However, only thirty percent of the four hundred acres in the park are utilized, and it remains to be seen if the park will ever reach its anticipated potential.

And what of the future?

Well, until that far-distant time, when a sixty-mile-long bridge or causeway is built to connect northern Cape Breton and Port aux Basques, the town of North Sydney will always remain the official "Gateway to Newfoundland and Labrador." And I see nothing wrong with that!

Chapter 1

The Waterfront and Business District

PLANT HOUSE, c.1876

Samuel Plant (1787–1881), often referred to as North Sydney's first businessman, built this imposing two-story house around 1834, with stone imported from England. It stood on the corner of what is now Marine Atlantic's parking lot, and plans were underway to have it declared a Historic Property when it was unceremoniously torn down by Canadian National Marine in the late 1980s to extend a parking lot. His original general store (circa 1826) was located at the corner of Queen and Regent Streets, near Smelt Brook. In addition to his store, he also had a sawmill and a very busy wharf, which was used by sailing ships from all parts of the world.

At a Town Council meeting in 1887 the three-mile-long main thoroughfare in North Sydney, previously known as Water Street, was officially divided into three sections. Queen Street extended from the town boundary at Musgrave Lane (Munro Park) to the old post office on the corner of Peppett Street. Commercial Street ran from this corner to the Newfoundland Ferry Terminal. Purves Street, named after the town's first mayor, William Purves, stretched from the ferry wharf to Northside General Hospital.

French Dreadnaught, c.1860

This French warship, belching smoke, is an excellent example of the increased marine traffic that stopped in North Sydney after the invention of the steam engine. These new engines required large amounts of coal, and the coal mines on the north side of the harbour could provide a ready supply. Notice, however, that this three-masted warship with her large smoking funnel was a hybrid design, with both sails and steam. It would be another twenty or thirty years before sail power would become obsolete. Although St. Pierre and Miquelon were the only French possessions in eastern Canada, the French navy kept a high profile off the East Coast.

North Sydney's Water Street (Commercial Street), 1886

In this interesting photo, looking west, you can see four of the town's prominent landmarks. The large smokestack in the left foreground marks the location of the North Sydney Marine Railway, which started operation in 1866. In the near distance, on the right-hand side, is the massive stone bulk of the brand new (1886) Post Office and Customs Office, on the corner of Commercial and Peppett Streets. Immediately behind it is the steeple of St. Matthew-Wesley United Church, built in 1899. In the distance can be seen Calvary Baptist Church, on the corner of Park and Beech streets, which opened in 1876. Notice the wooden sidewalk on the right side of the street! Unpaved streets resulted in very muddy and wet conditions whenever it rained, or in times of snowmelts.

Blacksmith and Carriage Builders, 1891

Looking quite pleased with himself, as well he should be, D. W. MacKinnon ran one of the more profitable blacksmith shops on the north-side. Long before the age of the automobile, his staff of twelve, including two young apprentice boys in the front, offered a wide range of products and services. Horseshoes, harness equipment, iron nails and bolts, and hand-made wagons and fancy carriages were all available. Their shop was located on the corner of Regent and Queen Streets.

Old Coal Pier and Church from Downtown, 1900

A very muddy thoroughfare, taken from the corner of Court and Commercial Streets, before the streetcar tracks were laid in 1901. In the background you can see the original coal pier, built in 1834, and the roof and steeple of St. Joseph's Catholic Church on Convent Street. The large Gannon building, at the lower end of Blower's Street, is visible at rear left. It was demolished in 2005.

John D. Steele & Sons Monument Works, c.1900

John D. Steele was born in 1868 in Long Island, Cape Breton. As a young man he went to Boston, where he learned his trade as an apprentice with a stonemason. Returning to Cape Breton, he started his own business in 1896. This picture shows his second shop, which was located on the water side of Commercial Street, in front of the present day Ballast Ground. In the early 1930s the business moved across the street, and moved again in 1948 to its present location on William Street. Still in operation as a family business after more than one hundred years, the company works with marble, granite, and bronze, to produce headstones, monuments, and other construction-related material. Examples of the Steeles' work can be found at the old post office in Sydney Mines and the Royal Bank of Canada in North Sydney. A magnificent sandstone lion, on a pedestal on the Esplanade in Sydney, was made at this shop. It once graced the façade of the Royal Bank of Canada in Sydney.

COMMERCIAL STREET, 1900

A very muddy Queen Street with the steeple of St. Matthew–Wesley United Church on the left. Behind it are the old post office and the Royal Albert Hall. The three-storey building on the right was the Bethany Mission, an evangelistic mission church used by traveling ministers to preach the Gospel. From 1918 to 1968 it was in use as the Sailor's Institute, a place for visiting sailors and fishermen to gather and socialize. It later became the Masonic Temple.

COAL AND IRON ORE PIERS, c.1905

Between 1902 and 1903 the Nova Scotia Steel and Coal Company, from New Glasgow, built three new wooden shipping piers at the foot of Goat Hill. The two on the left, the "high" pier and the "low" pier, replaced a single coal shipping pier that had been built in 1834. The new piers enabled the steel company to ship coal produced in Sydney Mines, as that town does not have a harbour. The "high" coal pier was one thousand feet long, and stood sixty feet above the high-water mark. It was designed to load large ocean going freighters and was capable of loading seven thousand tons of coal in a six-hour period.

The "low" coal pier was thirteen hundred feet long and stood thirty-four feet above high water. It was designed to load smaller vessels, such as schooners, barques, and brigantines.

In 1902, Nova Scotia Steel and Coal also started construction of a modern steel plant in Sydney Mines. As there is no iron ore on Cape Breton Island, they built a "stand-alone" iron ore pier, seen on the right side of the picture, in order to import iron ore from Bell Island, Newfoundland.

The iron ore pier was 1140 feet long and stood forty-two feet above high water. The unusual device on top is a moveable, steam-powered derrick, with winches at each end of its elongated arm. These were used to lift the heavy loads of iron ore from ships arriving from Newfoundland.

SHIPPING PIERS FROM THE HARBOUR, C.1905

A very rare photograph of the three new shipping piers as seen from the water. The iron ore pier is on the left, while the “low” and “high” coal piers are on the right side of the picture. A schooner and a small coastal freighter are tied up at the “low” coal pier. Goat Hill is in the background.

SS *Modiva* at Iron Ore Pier, c.1905

Two giant movable steam-powered derricks prepare to off-load iron ore from Newfoundland for use at the new steel plant in Sydney Mines.

Iron Ore Pier and People, 1905

A group of rather daring individuals pose on the superstructure of one of the steam-powered derricks. A second derrick is in the background, while the high and low coal piers can be seen on the left.

Schooner at Low Coal Pier, c.1937

This dynamic photograph by Nelson Rice is full of fascinating detail with regard to the operation of a coal pier. The supporting structure of this pier is made entirely from wood—there was no iron or steel used in construction, other than nails and supporting clamps!

There are no coal deposits to speak of in either Newfoundland or Prince Edward Island, so both areas depended to a large part on imports of coal from Cape Breton Island. It was common practice for schooners to drop off a load of fish in North Sydney, and load up with coal for a return voyage to Newfoundland or PEI.

This schooner is burdened with a heavy load of coal—visible on deck—that was loaded via the coal chute in the upper-right corner of the photograph. The coal cars from the mines in Sydney Mines would be shunted out on the coal pier, their bottoms would open, and the coal would drop down the chute and into a waiting vessel. This schooner is so weighed down with coal that there is only about four feet of "freeboard" between the water and the deck rail of the boat. Two dories, centre and right, which would normally be carried on deck, will be placed on top of the coal for their return voyage.

ALBERT HOTEL, 1906

This impressive-looking building with thirty rooms, located on Summer Street, went through several name changes before being destroyed by fire in 1950. Built in 1876 as the Western Union Hotel, it served as a boarding house for non-married employees of the Western Union Cable Office. It was later sold and renamed the Presto House. In 1895 it was sold again and renamed the North Sydney Hotel. By 1900 it had been sold for a fourth time and was now known as the Albert Hotel. It was considered one of the finest hotels on the north side of Sydney Harbour.

COMMERCIAL STREET LOOKING WEST, 1907

The imposing façade of the five-year-old Vooght Brothers Building dominates the right side of this excellent photograph. Behind it is the Royal Café, on the present site of the Canton Restaurant. The three-storey building on the left has a sign that reads "Boarding & Lodging," while the sign on the two-storey place behind it simply states "Billiards."

This picture is unique due to the presence of an electric streetcar (tramcar), which ran on iron rails. Electricity from overhead wires was used to provide a relatively quiet form of transit. The Cape Breton Electric Tramway & Power Company was incorporated in 1900. In 1901, the company's name was changed to The Cape Breton Electric Company. It operated a local street railway service in Sydney and a separate (not physically connected) six- mile street railway line between North Sydney and Sydney Mines. The company also operated a ferry service between Sydney and North Sydney.

Cogan's Livery Stables, Blowers Street, c.1906

A charming photograph of a family business that operated in North Sydney in the late nineteenth and early twentieth centuries. In the late 1880s, Patrick Cogan emigrated from Ireland and settled in Leitches Creek. Shortly after, he moved into town and opened a livery stable on the site of the present day downtown Tim Hortons outlet. Two of his four sons, James and Luke, continued to operate the business until the late 1920s. To the right of the building you can plainly see the "high" and "low" coal piers in Ward 4.

In the days before the widespread use of motorized vehicles, livery stables provided a very important service for the town and surrounding rural areas. Individuals, whether residents or visitors, could rent a horse and carriage by the hour, day, or week. Business people could rent a horse and wagon to deliver goods to customers, or pick up passengers and freight from the train station and the various wharves along the waterfront. Regular service was also provided from the downtown area to Christie's wharf in Little Bras D'Or, which had ferry connections with various points around the Bras D'Or Lakes.

COMMERCIAL STREET LOOKING EAST (BELMONT HOTEL), 1914

The woman on the left, dressed in a long skirt, is standing at the corner of Commercial Street and Archibald Avenue. The building directly in front of her, with the wide verandahs on the first and second floors, is the twenty-eight-room Belmont Hotel, which was built in the late 1870s. In the days before microphones, visiting politicians and other dignitaries would often use the second- floor balcony as a place from which to give speeches, announce election results, and make public announcements. The hotel, which was the preferred stopover for commercial or business travelers, was destroyed by fire in 1929. The store on the extreme right is Bent & Cohoon Hardware, while the Vendome Hotel is second from the right.

COMMERCIAL STREET LOOKING EAST (THOMPSON AND SUTHERLAND HARDWARE), 1914

Taken from the corner of Commercial and Caledonia Streets on the eve of World War One, this interesting photo plainly shows the connection from the tram car on rails to the overhead electric wire. The horse and wagon on the right is also a reminder that this old-fashioned combination was still a primary means of transportation for most people who lived in the surrounding rural areas. Notice as well the wooden sidewalks, and the awnings in front of the stores on the left to protect them from the early morning sun.

The large building on the left is Thompson and Sutherland Hardware, a New Glasgow firm which first set up shop in North Sydney in 1868. This store, their second at the same location, opened in 1901 and continued to operate until 1970. The firm ran a successful business at this downtown location for 102 years! They also operated a foundry on the other side of the railway tracks at the end of King Street, by the North Sydney Mall.

I can still fondly remember, about 1957, standing in front of a large window at Thompson and Sutherland's early in the evening, along with a fairly substantial group of people, watching a program on a small black and white television that had been placed on a stand inside the store. We were amazed at this new invention, even though we could not hear anything.

HMS *DRAKE*, 1916

Built in 1902 for Britain's Royal Navy, this armoured cruiser was considered to be one of the fastest warships in the world, with a top speed of twenty-three knots. For three years (1915–1917) it was an important part of Britain's North Atlantic Squadron and, like most other warships of the time, made frequent stops in North Sydney in order to obtain coal for its steam engines. In 1917, at the height of World War One, HMS *Drake* was hit by an enemy torpedo off the coast of Northern Ireland. It sank a few hours later, with a loss of nineteen lives. More than 870 other crew members survived. This ship was almost as large as the present Newfoundland ferry—the *Caribou*!

THOMPSON'S FOUNDRY, c.1916

In 1903, the A. C. Thompson Company built this large industrial structure at the end of King Street, just across the railway tracks. With two rows of large windows to provide natural lighting, it produced furnaces, stoves, kitchen ranges, and various other iron products. In 1949, the foundry was purchased by Angel Manufacturing and Supply Limited, which continued to operate it in a diminished capacity until the mid-1960s.

On the left, in the background, is the tall, circular outline of a small blast furnace, where molten pig iron was produced. The workers, alone or in pairs, would carry the molten metal from the furnace to the rectangular moulds, made from very fine sand, visible on the right side of the picture. The hollow interior of these moulds represented the form of a particular piece of metal, such as a stove top or furnace part. When the molten metal cooled, the metal boxes containing the moulds were turned upside down, and the sand was removed to reveal a "metal casting."

My grandfather, Hector Michael MacLean (Hector Mick), is in the second row, second from the right. This was dangerous, backbreaking work, done under sweltering conditions of high heat and humidity, and Hector worked at it for more than fifty years. I would often visit him at work on my way home from school and was always impressed by the workmanship exhibited by these men. They were tradesmen in the best sense of the term and took great pride in what they produced.

Pouring Iron at Thompson's Foundry, c.1916

Sparks fly as molten iron is poured into small, hand-held, cast-iron ladles. These ladles would then be carried over to and poured into waiting moulds. Needless to say, this was extremely dangerous work, with the constant possibility of serious, crippling burns. Notice the lack of safety goggles, clothing, or protective equipment of any kind. The reason: molten iron would instantly burn through any protective device, and the men preferred to maintain ease of movement in these hazardous situations.

Assembly Line— Thompson's Foundry, c.1916

Coal and wood-burning stoves and furnaces were assembled by hand for shipment to all parts of the Maritime Provinces and Newfoundland.

Cars on Parade, c.1920

This photograph offers a fascinating juxtaposition of three land-based forms of transportation used in North Sydney immediately after World War One: on the right, a total of sixteen gasoline-powered automobiles, or motor-cars; on the left, two horse-powered wagons, which by this date were rapidly becoming restricted to the rural areas surrounding the town; in the centre, an electric streetcar (tramcar), which used electricity to provide a relatively quiet form of transit between North Sydney and Sydney Mines. Notice, in the background, the coal pier and St. Joseph's Convent with the cupola on top.

COMMERCIAL STREET, C.1920 This picture gives a rare view of the overhead wires that provided the electricity to operate the streetcars, or tramcars. Notice the tram tracks under the car in the centre of the picture.

OLD POST OFFICE AND ROYAL ALBERT HALL, 1910

North Sydney's first post office opened in 1851, though its exact location remains a bit of a mystery. In those days, the mail arrived by boat from Halifax or Europe. In the often stormy winter months, however, especially when the pack ice was in the harbour, the mail came overland from Halifax, carried by one or more Mi'kmaq on snowshoes. The second post office was built in 1872, in a lane off lower Court Street. The third, on the corner of Commercial and Peppett Streets, was an imposing three-storey stone edifice opened in 1886. The first floor contained the post office; the second, the customs and excise office; the third, a custodian's apartment. This building remained in use for seventy-five years, until it was finally closed and demolished in 1961. Today, a one-level block of doctors' offices stands on the same spot, across from the Irving Station.

The Royal Albert Hall, named after Queen Victoria's husband, was a three-storey structure that opened in 1890. The hall on the first floor was the scene of many of the town's social events including concerts, plays, minstrel shows, and other forms of light entertainment. The second floor was used by the Sons of Temperance, an organization whose members promised not to touch intoxicating liquor of any kind. This unique institution held its first meeting in New York, in 1842, in the appropriately named Teetotallers Hall. The Royal Albert Lodge, a men's fraternal organization, used the third floor for meetings and social gatherings. In 1905 the building was bought by the Salvation Army. Today, it is the location of a new one-storey office building.

Getting Ready for Paving, 1929

In this interesting picture taken at the corner of Lorne and Queen Streets, a bulldozer tows a primitive, non-motorized grader. The grader spreads gravel to provide a solid footing for the cement that will be poured later. All controls on the grader were operated by hand, including raising and lowering of the large blade underneath the machine. Notice the wooden forms on the side of the road. The first streets paved in North Sydney were Queen, Commercial, and Purves.

POST OFFICE CORNER JUST BEFORE PAVING, 1929

The massive, fortress-like post office looms on the right, while the steeple and part of St. Matthew–Wesley United Church is visible just behind it. On the left, where the Irving gas station stands today, are the showroom and gas pumps of Daniel J. Campbell's Auto Dealership, the first in North Sydney. Campbell opened this business, which sold Chevrolet cars, in the early 1920s.

Aerial View from Musgrave Lane, 1931

This panoramic view shows the entire town of North Sydney from the southwest. The coal piers dominate the waterfront, and the gentle curves of the railroad tracks can be followed from Gannon Road (centre left) to the lower right-hand side of the picture.

AERIAL VIEW TO GANNON ROAD, 1931

In this low-level photograph, looking north towards Gannon Road, you can clearly see Pierce Street (left centre) and Pleasant Street (right centre). Several landmarks are also visible: St. John's Anglican Church and Hall, on the corner of King and Pleasant Streets; St. Joseph's Catholic Church, on the corner of Pierce Street and Archibald Avenue; the Western Union Cable Office, Court Street; the long narrow outline of the Canadian National Railway Newfoundland freight shed, on the corner of Blowers and Station Streets; Lily Lake, upper left. The large, open area at the corner of Archibald Avenue and Stanley Street is the Alexandra Tennis Club, which had three courts. Named after Queen Alexandra, the wife of King Edward VII, the club opened in 1901 and continued to operate until after World War Two.

ALLEN ICE COMPANY—MUSGRAVE LANE, 1935

Ice from nearby Pottle's Lake is loaded into a large barn, where it will be covered with straw and sawdust to keep it from melting. In the days before electric or gas refrigerators, most homes had an ice box to keep food chilled. Blocks of ice would be delivered to homeowners by horse and wagon in the warmer months. There was also a large commercial business in delivering ice to the Newfoundland ferries and the various fish plants that lined the waterfront. The Allen Ice Company dated back to 1907, when Charles Allen started to cut ice on Pottle's Lake and sell it around town.

Left to right: Jim Allen, John Rogers, Percy Brown, Harry Moore, Elburn Allen, and unknown.

Ballast Grounds Connected, 1960

This large pile of rocks and boulders was built up over a period of one hundred years (1834– 1934). Schooners and other ships coming to North Sydney for a load of coal, would dump their excess ballast at this spot before proceeding to the local coal piers. By the early 1950s, the rocks and boulders representing more than one hundred years of ballast had become physically connected to the town's waterfront. A gravel road soon gave access to this rocky peninsula, which before long had a series of wharfs along its perimeter. Today, local fishing boats tie up here during the winter months.

North Sydney's Fiftieth Anniversary, 1935

On the fiftieth anniversary of North Sydney's incorporation as a town, many parades and social activities took place throughout the summer months. This fascinating picture shows the original Northern Yacht Club building (now Rollie's Wharf), with a large ship loading coal at the "high" coal pier in the background. Automobiles line up to watch boat races, while a coastal steamer waits in the harbour. Due to problems with coal dust from the piers, and increasing ship traffic, the Northern Yacht Club moved to its present location near Kelly's Beach (Munro Park) in 1948.

Owl Drug Store, 1936

In this charming picture, the young winners of a contest sponsored by the drug store pose with their prizes. Unfortunately, we do not know the nature of the contest, or the identity of most of the prizewinners. However, Albert Jesty, Jr. is the young lad seated on the left with a new pair of skates, and Bernie Yorke is seated on the right. The boy standing on the right, in a flying jacket and leather helmet, has a new hockey stick, while the two young ladies standing on the left are obviously quite proud of their new dolls.

JESTY'S BAKERY, 1937

In 1921 Albert Jesty started this family business on the north corner of Caledonia and Stanley Streets. Within ten years it was the largest bakery on the north-side, with sales all over Cape Breton Island, the eastern part of mainland Nova Scotia, and the west coast of Newfoundland. A full range of products was produced, including various types of bread, biscuits, cakes, and pastries. A fleet of horse-drawn wagons, later supplemented by trucks, delivered the fresh product to local customers, while other parts of the island were served by road, rail, or steamship. When Albert died in the early 1950s, his three sons took over the business. Stan, Pat, and Albert Jesty continued the tradition until the bakery was destroyed by fire in February, 1957.

Notice the loaves of bread on metal racks, in the doorway on the right-hand side of the building, ready to be loaded into waiting trucks and the solitary wagon. Stan Jesty Sr. is seated on the barrel, while his brother Pat rests his right elbow on the headlight of the centre truck. Their father Albert leans on the door. The inscription on the side of the wagon reads: "Here is your staff of life—Jesty's Bread."

I have vivid memories of my brother John and I, Jack MacKay, Peter and David Miller, and Stan Jesty Jr., loading bread and cakes into the trucks in the evening, to be delivered early the next morning. We were rewarded with a few loaves of bread, or fresh cakes with lots of icing! The perpetually warm attic of Jesty's Bakery was also a great place to play on a rainy afternoon or a cold day in the winter. I must confess, after all these years, to filling my pockets from the raisin barrel, whenever I had the opportunity!

Landing Cod at Nickerson's Wharf, c.1941

A vivid reminder of the days when the cod stocks were plentiful, and schooners were the vessel of choice for fishing on the Grand Banks of Newfoundland. In this photo, the codfish visible on the dock have been off-loaded by crew members using pitchforks. Although small-scale fish processing had been carried on in North Sydney all through the 1800s, it was not until 1918 that the first major fish plant was set up.

Recreational Fishing at Nickerson's Wharf, c.1941

With the end of World War One in 1918, the fishing industry on Canada's east coast rapidly expanded to fill an increasing international demand for fish products. As a result, four large fish-processing companies opened in North Sydney over the next twenty years. The first was Leonard Brothers Limited. In 1918, they built a brand-new fish plant at the former Farquhar's Wharf. After fire destroyed that operation in 1950, a new fish plant was built on Salter's Wharf, located at the end of Regent Street across from the Smelt Brook. In 1945 Leonard Brothers became part of National Sea Products Limited.

In 1920, the appropriately named Cape Breton Cold Storage Company built a facility that was capable of freezing and storing more than one million pounds of fish! It was destroyed by fire in 1932. Three years later, in 1935, the third fish plant opened under the name H. B. Nickerson and Sons Limited. A large part of that business was lost to fire in 1969, but was quickly rebuilt.

The last fish-processing firm, North Sydney Agencies, opened in 1937. It later became part of the Thomas W. Sainthill Company.

North Sydney Marine Railway—Ship in Cradle, 1944

What is a marine railway? When this family business started in 1865, it consisted of a large wooden cradle on iron tracks which was attached to a steam engine by a steel cable. The tracks extended out under the water. A ship needing repairs would sail into the cradle, which would then be winched up out of the harbour. When repairs were completed, the process was reversed, and the ship sailed away.

When the Archibald family built the Marine Railway, they actually constructed two such cradles. The large cradle, built to support "square-rigged" sailing ships, could handle up to eighteen hundred tons. A smaller cradle would look after repairs to fishing schooners and other local craft. The company also provided full repair services including carpentry shops, painters, masts and rigging supplies, and a machine shop.

Marine Railway— Men Working c.1944

In this fascinating photo, men are working on a wooden coastal steamer, from the west coast of Newfoundland. Rotten planks in the hull are being replaced, while a welder on the left makes repairs to an iron strip on the bow. Part of the cradle can be seen on the far left.

Jo Bugden, Diver, 1944

Joe was one of several experienced divers with the Marine Railway. With World War Two in full swing, there was plenty of work for divers in North Sydney. In addition to warships and boats damaged in convoy, the Newfoundland ferry and coastal boats and local fishing schooners all required yearly maintenance. A new responsibility was also maintaining the anti-submarine net that stretched across the mouth of Sydney Harbour.

Cenotaph and Memorial Park and Two Guns, 1944

On Remembrance Day (November 11), 1929, this granite war memorial to the town's dead of World War One (1914–1918) was unveiled on lower Archibald Avenue. Fifty-one names are listed on the monument, along with the major battlefields of the "War To End All Wars." In the years after World War Two (1939–1945), two granite slabs with the names of sixty-eight local men killed in that conflict were placed on each side of the entrance to the Town Hall on Commercial Street. These slabs were later removed and placed to flank the present cenotaph. The gun is a large World War One artillery cannon. At the outbreak of World War Two, this gun, and many more from around the province were shipped to the Sydney Steel Plant where they were melted down and turned into iron and steel for new weapons.

Fishing Schooners at Anchor, 1916

By the early 1800s North Sydney was well-known as an important Maritime fishing port. This reputation was only enhanced with the opening of the coal-shipping pier in 1834, and the arival of many internaitonal vessels in the local harbour. By the 1850s fishing boats from all over the Maritimes and Newfoundland would often call here to off-load fish and pick up supplies. By the 1880s fishing fleets of up to 300 schooners from Gloucester, Massachusetts, would often stop in for supplies and a well-deserved rest from the rigors of fishing on the Grand Banks of Newfoundland. This pattern continued until the start of World War One in 1914.

Portuguese Four-masted Fishing Vessels, c.1948

For well over a hundred years, from the 1870s to the 1970s, the town saw regular visits by the Portuguese fishing fleet. Known as the "White Fleet" due to the colour of their sails and hulls, the fleet left Portugal each spring to fish off Nova Scotia, Newfoundland and Labrador, Greenland, and Saint Pierre.

Some personal memories, from my school years, of the Portuguese White Fleet:

They used to wash their clothes in the brook that ran through Plant's field, where Marine Atlantic is today, and then hang them to dry on local fences or on the grass;

They would collect Simpson's and Eaton's catalogues to take home to their wives and girlfriends, who would then be aware of the latest fashions and styles from North America;

Their exceptional ability to play soccer, and do tricks with a soccer ball, when we were just being exposed to this foreign game in our gym classes;

How well-behaved, deferential, and friendly the Portuguese sailors were, when ashore.

They seldom seemed to have any money, but were always smiling and happy, and always kind to children.

Men and Dories, c.1947 A tranquil, haunting scene, this beautifully composed image suggests the timeless beauty of a safe anchorage, which the port of North Sydney has provided for hundreds of years.

Vooght Brothers' Store Under Construction, 1902

John Vooght, who was born in England, opened his first small store in North Sydney in 1862. He was later joined by his two brothers, Tom and James, and in 1873 the three opened a large general store on the corner of Commercial and Court Streets. At that time it was the largest commercial building on Cape Breton Island. When it was destroyed by fire in 1902, the brothers built a larger four-storey business on the same site, now the location of the Bank of Nova Scotia.

In this interesting photograph of the new store under construction, you can just make out the scaffolding around the exterior of the building, as well as the large water tower on its top. The Vooght brothers also operated a substantial wholesale business, with their own wharf and two warehouses located on the waterfront.

Vooght Brothers' Store with Staff, 1914

All thirty-three staff, nineteen women and fourteen men, line up for a group photo in front of their store. Constructed of brick and stone, it was the largest department store east of Montreal. It also had two elevators, probably a first in the Maritime Provinces, one for passengers and one for freight. Notice the name "Vooght Brothers" carved above the door and the brass "hitching rail" at waist level along the front of the store, used, of course, to tie up your horse!

Groceries and Chinaware, 1914

The ground floor of the store had an open concept, with sixteen massive Doric-style pillars supporting the considerable weight of the three upper floors. The five departments on this floor were separated from one another by eight-foot-high wooden dividers. These included Shoes, Men's and Women's Clothing, Groceries and Chinaware, Notions (hair ribbons, handkerchiefs, hat pins, etc.), and the quaintly-named Gentlemen's Furnishings, with socks, ties, and a wide selection of fancy umbrellas.

Shoe Department, 1914

Located at the far right of the ground floor, this department usually contained at least five thousand pairs of shoes! Glass display cases on the left showcased the latest styles in footwear, for both women and men, while the courteous staff made sure that the shoes or boots were properly fitted. A fitting often involved accurate measurements of the contours of an individual's foot—service that is rather hard to come by in today's large and impersonal department stores. In 1929, this section of the store became the town's official outlet for the Nova Scotia Liquor Commission. Notice, above each counter, a rectangular system of wires running off towards the back of the store. Bills of sale and monetary payments were placed in little metal boxes which were carried along these wire tracks to the mezzanine located at the back of the first floor. Here, in this elevated gallery, cashiers made change and sent the transaction back to the customer. The mezzanine can be seen at the back of this photograph.

MODERN DAY VOOGHT BUILDING, 1972

The Vooght Building as most of us remember it. From the left: Wong's Café; Grant's Jewelers;

Herald Stationers; Simpsons-Sears; Liquor Store (Nova Scotia Liquor Commission). By this time the brickwork on the upper floors had started to deteriorate, and a special gutter had been placed between the first and second floors to catch any falling bricks or debris.

Grant's Jewelers Store had been in operation for more than one hundred years, since 1871, although not always at this location. Herald Stationers, which started out in 1872 as a newspaper (The *North Sydney Herald*) and commercial printing operation, moved into the Vooght Building in 1947. The business had been purchased in 1935 by Charlie Miller, a recent graduate of Dalhousie Law School, and continued as a stationery store and print shop until the mid-1970s. Simpsons-Sears arrived in the 1960s, and the town's liquor store had been located in the far corner since 1929.

Chapter 2

Trans-Atlantic Telegraph Cable

CABLE OFFICE STAFF, 1904

Staff at their telegraph cubicles at the "old" Western Union office on Commercial Street (now Salter–Ratchford Insurance). This scene is eerily reminiscent of a modern-day call centre, with its computer cubicles and attendant supervisors hovering in the background.

Left to right: George Moffatt, Jack MacKenna, William Robson, Frank Maynard, Stan Earle, Ernest Angel, Howard McLearn, O.B. Saunders, Cliff Kelly, Len Moffatt, Alf Gunn, L.W. Wilson, Win Bedwin, George Collings, Fred MacDonald, Aubrey Angel, Ruben Chislett, Fred Tait, Douglas Mitchell, Fred Logan.

As knowledge of the once-common method of communicating via telegraph fades with each generation, a few definitions of the telegraph system are in order.

Telegraph: A system of electrical machines and instruments used to send and receive coded messages over a wire. Invented in New York and New Jersey by Samuel Morse and Alfred Vail between 1835–1838.

Telegraph Key: A simple device consisting of a metal lever, operating in an up-and-down motion, by which a telegrapher opened or closed an electrical switch, thus sending pulses of electricity along the telegraph wire.

Telegrapher: A person who sends and receives telegraph messages. Experienced telegraphers could transmit messages at speeds of up to thirty words a minute! Telegraphers often developed serious medical problems, accompanied by severe pain, with their wrists and forearms. In the late nineteenth and early twentieth centuries this condition was known as "telegrapher's paralysis" or "glass arm." Today we refer to it as "carpal tunnel syndrome."

Telegram: A telegraph message that requires immediate delivery. There were three forms of telegram: The day letter was a popular fifty-word message that would be delivered within twenty-four hours for a cheap rate. The night letter was an overnight message that would be delivered by early the next morning, anywhere in Canada or the United States. And finally, the night message was the shortest and cheapest type of overnight communication.

Morse Code: A telegraphic message system whereby letters and numbers are represented by a series of dots, dashes, and spaces, or their equivalent sounds.

Western Union Telegraph Company: A union of eleven small telegraph firms in 1856, headquartered in Rochester, New York. It joined "western" and "eastern" companies together into one nationwide system. The company celebrated its 150th anniversary in 2001.

Western Union Christmas Dinner, 1908

In this quaint picture, the seventeen staff members of the local Western Union Telegraph Office gather at a local hotel for a formal banquet on Boxing Day.

Left to right: Robert Parker, Frank Maynard, George Moffatt, Fred Logan, Cliff Kelly, Arthur Partridge, Ernest Angel, James Coppin, William Robson, A.J. Coppin, I.H. Angel, T.A. Colwell, Doug Mitchell, Bren Hennessy, Alf Gunn, Fred MacDonald, James Kenna.

Lloyd's Cove Landing, Sydney Mines, 1954

The small concrete building to the right of the "Cables" sign marks the spot where the trans-Atlantic telegraph cable came ashore on the north side of Sydney Harbour. It was transferred here from Aspy Bay in northern Cape Breton in 1875. By the time of World War Two, most trans-Atlantic underwater cables bypassed Newfoundland and came directly to Cape Breton.

Centerville, Laying the Cable, 1913

The cable from Lloyd's Cove to North Sydney was laid in a four-foot-deep trench and covered with several layers of wooden planks. Notice the railway tracks on the right side of the road, used by the electric tramcars of the Cape Breton Electric Company. The six-mile-long rail system made it easy and comfortable for people to travel between the two towns in the days before automobiles became common.

First Western Union Cable Office, 1913

When the underwater trans-Atlantic telegraph cable was successfully completed in 1858, it stretched for more than two thousand miles from the west coast of Ireland to the east coast of Newfoundland. It then went overland to Port aux Basques, under the Cabot Strait to Aspy Bay in northern Cape Breton, and then overland again, by way of Ingonish and Baddeck, to the Strait of Canso.

In 1875, the Cape Breton end of the cable was transferred from Aspy Bay to the north side of Sydney Harbour, and a new cable office was built in North Sydney. The cable actually came ashore in Lloyd's Cove, Sydney Mines. From there it ran underground for three miles, following the Shore Road between the two towns until it reached the new office in North Sydney.

This new facility, on the corner of Commercial and Union Streets, had twenty-five employees under the direction of W.S. Snyder. By 1900, twenty-five years later, more than sixty people worked at the cable office, under very crowded conditions.

This building was sold in 1916 to Joseph Salter & Sons for five thousand dollars. It still stands across from the Irving station and is now the home of Salter–Ratchford Insurance.

Western Union Branch Office, 1913

By 1910, working conditions had become so crowded at the main cable office that a decision was made to open a branch office in the heart of downtown North Sydney. Located on the water side, opposite Archibald Avenue, the wooden building in the centre of this photo also held the office of the harbour master.

The impressive stone building on the left was built in 1901 for the Union Bank of Halifax. In 1910 the Union Bank was purchased by the Royal Bank of Canada, and this became the local outlet of the Royal Bank. In 1950 this structure was torn down, and a brand new bank was built on the same location.

The store on the right of the photo has a sign which reads: "Jenkins & Gillis [no relation to the author], Reliable Home Furnishings."

NEW CABLE OFFICE UNDER CONSTRUCTION, COURT STREET, 1913

By 1913, the total number of telegraph messages transmitted during an eight-hour shift had increased to over ten thousand, and Western Union decided to build a new and much larger office building. The company purchased land at the upper end of Court Street and construction started immediately. This new brick building, built like a fortress with walls at least three feet thick, was built by Frank Redding, a local contractor, at a cost of eighty thousand dollars (approximately $1.5 million today). The outer walls of the new building were later covered with a thick layer of cement.

In 1914, Western Union had approximately twenty-five thousand telegraph offices around the world. However, when the new North Sydney office opened in December of that year, it was considered to be the most modern and technologically advanced of them all, with machines and instrumentation that would be worth well over one million dollars in today's terms. A total of nine trans-Atlantic cables now arrived in North Sydney, capable of handling and transmitting thirty thousand messages each day! When Western Union shut down the operation in 1962, the building was purchased by St. Joseph's Parish to be used as a parish centre. It stands vacant today. It is such a massive structure that the cost of tearing it down far exceeds the value of the land on which it stands.

Store House, 1920

New two-storey brick store house, which served as a small warehouse for supplies such as batteries, morse keys, and various types of electrical equipment. Its roof, like that of the cable office, was made of copper sheets.

Cable Office— Main Floor, c.1924

At least twenty-nine staff members are visible in this panoramic shot taken from the north corner of the second floor. Among the electrical machines in this picture were an early form of "ticker," a telegraphic machine that records stock market reports or news on a thin paper tape (ticker-tape). Sports scores also came in to the office on the "ticker," and the men who worked there would know the results of important games before anyone else on the island! A strict dress code was followed at the cable office and male employees were required to wear suits with white shirts and dark ties. The manager's office, with the large expanse of glass, is in the centre rear.

Chapter 3

Transportation

SS *BRUCE*, MAIDEN VOYAGE, 1898

At approximately 11 P.M., on the night of June 30, 1898, the steamship SS *Bruce* slipped away from the wharf, manoeuvred around the dangerous rocks at the entrance to Port aux Basques Harbour, and entered the darkened confines of the Cabot Strait. Early the next morning, shortly after daybreak, the ship sailed into the harbour at North Sydney. The two British Dominions in North America were now linked by a scheduled ferry service that would provide three round-trip crossings per week between Canada and Newfoundland.

The fifty or so passengers on that first scheduled crossing had left St. John's the previous evening. Facing a train journey of up to thirty hours, they were nevertheless enthusiastic to be part of the first scheduled train service between the east and west coasts of Newfoundland. The train covered the 550-mile distance in twenty-seven hours, arriving in Port aux Basques late the next evening. The SS *Bruce* was waiting.

Built in Glasgow, Scotland, the new ferry's appointments and accommodation were of the highest calibre, comparable to any large passenger ship on the trans-Atlantic run. Its speed, its ice-handling capability, and its all-steel design were far superior to any other vessel on the east coast of Canada. For the next thirteen years the *Bruce* faithfully went about its business, carrying more than three hundred thousand passengers in safety and comfort across the Cabot Strait. Then, in the early morning hours of March 24, 1911, its luck ran out.

With 123 sleeping passengers on board, the ship ran hard aground on a rocky ledge on the outskirts of the little fishing town of Louisbourg on the east coast of Cape Breton. The *Bruce* had been diverted to this ice-free port because North Sydney was icebound for some time. In the ensuing confusion and terror, five men attempting to launch one of the lifeboats were swept into the raging sea. Three of them were able to make their way back on board, while two others disappeared beneath the freezing waters and were lost.

Thanks to the heroic efforts of the *Bruce*'s crew and other passengers, all those left on board were safely put ashore and eventually made their way to Louisbourg. Nothing, however, could be done for their doomed ship. With the subsequent break-up of the SS *Bruce*, on the ice-covered rocks off Louisbourg, the first era of regular scheduled passenger and freight service between Canada and Newfoundland came to an end.

SS *BRUCE* ON THE ROCKS, MARCH 24, 1911

In this dramatic photograph, the first Newfoundland–Nova Scotia ferry, coated in ice, lies on a jagged ledge between Scatarie Island and Main-a-Dieu, just a few miles from the safety of Louisbourg Harbour. Heavy seas and swells later that afternoon eventually caused the stricken vessel to break in two, and she was left to disintegrate on the rock-strewn coast.

Terminus Wharf and Customs Office, 1945

The end of the Canadian National Railway in eastern Canada. Two Newfoundland coastal boats are tied up on either side of the small freight shed. The large building on the right contains offices, waiting rooms, and Canada Customs. Since Newfoundland did not become part of Canada until 1949, all passengers arriving on the Newfoundland ferry would have to be processed by Canada Customs, as they were arriving from a foreign country! Notice the high coal pier on the extreme left of the picture.

Terminus Wharf in Winter, 1945

A massive ocean-going freighter, in port to replenish its coal bunkers, dominates this winter scene at the Newfoundland Terminus. The Newfoundland ferry is to the right of the freight shed, while five schooners are frozen in the ice, waiting for the start of the spring fishing season.

SS *KYLE* AT NORTH SYDNEY MARINE RAILWAY, 1920

Built in Scotland in 1913 for the Labrador service, the *Kyle's* hull was reinforced to operate in severe ice conditions. During World War One (1914–1918) the *Kyle* and its courageous crew carried men, materials, and war supplies from North Sydney (Canada) to Newfoundland (a British Dominion). Although there were several close calls with enemy submarines, its luck held, and it provided a vital service for the remainder of the war. In 1927, after fourteen years of service on the Cabot Strait, the sturdy *Kyle* was re-assigned to the role for which it was originally designed: the Labrador coastal service. The ship remained on the Labrador run for the next thirty-three years, until 1960, when it was sold to a Newfoundland firm.

For the next few years, the *Kyle* took men and supplies to the annual spring seal hunt off Labrador. However, in 1965 it sustained severe damage after hitting an iceberg and was forced to retire from active duty after an astounding fifty-two years at sea! Today, the *Kyle* can be seen in Harbour Grace, Newfoundland.

SS *Caribou*, 1940

Built in Holland in 1925 for the Newfoundland ferry service, the *Caribou* was 265 feet long and weighed 2200 tons. With a reinforced bow and unusually thick hull plates, it was built to handle the type of severe ice conditions that it would encounter each spring. It had a capacity of 155 first-class and 255 second-class passengers and set a new standard for comfort and convenience on the east coast.

The *Caribou's* social amenities included a co-ed social lounge and a smoking room for men only. It was the first vessel in the Newfoundland service to have steam-radiators in every cabin, as well as cold storage facilities for perishable cargo. It was also the first to have a piano on board! The ship was acclaimed on both sides of the Cabot Strait as the finest vessel ever to serve on the Newfoundland run.

On the night of October 14, 1942, the *Caribou* slipped away from the wharf at North Sydney and pointed its bow in the direction of Newfoundland, one hundred miles away. The ship was unescorted. On board were 238 passengers and crew, while below were military supplies for the war effort in Newfoundland. Later that night, at approximately 3:50 A.M., the ship was rocked by an explosion that almost lifted it out of the water. Severely damaged, it immediately developed a serious list to port, while pandemonium reigned above and below decks.

A second torpedo struck shortly after, and within five minutes the *Caribou* was gone. The pride of the Newfoundland ferry service, a proud vessel that had served faithfully for almost eighteen years, had disappeared beneath the cold waters of the Cabot Strait taking 137 of the passengers and crew with it. There were 101 survivors, most of whom were not rescued until several hours after the sinking. Because of wartime security, it took three days for the local newspapers to release the story. The residents of North Sydney and Port aux Basques, however, were well aware of what had happened within a matter of hours. The *Caribou* carried a crew of forty-six, most of whom lived in Port aux Basques. Of these, thirty-one went down with their ship.

SS *Cabot Strait*, 1949

The *Cabot Strait,* built in Scotland in 1947, was the fourth in a series of ships that had all been specifically ordered for service with the Newfoundland ferry service. Like the others, it was first and foremost a ship designed to carry passengers, cargo, animals, and the Royal Mail.

However, like the two *Bruces* and the original *Caribou,* it was much more than just a working ship. The walls of its public areas glowed with the warmth of polished wood. The windows of these rooms contained superb examples of the rapidly disappearing art of stained glass. Brass objects such as portholes, door-steps, and fire extinguishers radiated an iridescent warmth that reflected many hours of polishing. The ship had "class"!

The *Cabot Strait* was 272 feet long and weighed 2046 tons. It had a crew of thirty-nine and could carry about 150 first- and second-class passengers. It operated on the Gulf run, between North Sydney and Port aux Basques, until the arrival of the car ferry *William Carson* in 1955. It then operated as a coastal boat and took over the Labrador service in 1960, when the *Kyle* retired. It continued to operate until the mid-1970s, when it officially retired.

MV *William Carson* Arrives in North Sydney, 1955

When Newfoundland became Canada's tenth province in 1949, the Newfoundland Railway, including all ferries and coastal boats, fell under the jurisdiction of Canadian National Railways.

Built in Montreal for Canadian National, and named after a famous doctor and politician in Newfoundland, the brand new ferry arrived in North Sydney in 1955 decked out in flags and other regalia.

The arrival of the *William Carson* represented a complete break with previous ferry designs, which had basically not changed since the turn of the century. All earlier ferries were ocean-going vessels, with hulls reinforced to handle the spring ice conditions in the Cabot Strait. They could accommodate slightly more than one hundred passengers, in first- and second-class cabins. All freight carried was hoisted on board by steam winches and lowered into cargo holds below decks. Any vehicles carried were hoisted on board and strapped down on the open decks!

The *William Carson*, however, was designed from the outset to be different from all previous ferries. Vehicles would now drive on board through openings in the side of the ship. Freight, usually in a metal container, would be loaded in the same manner.

The *William Carson* was huge. Over 350 feet long, it could carry over one hundred cars and trucks, as well as up to five hundred passengers. Its gross weight of 8,400 tons was more than four times the weight of the previous ferry. Launched in Quebec in 1953, it was the first Canadian-built ship to operate in the Newfoundland service. The *William Carson* first went into service between North Sydney and Argentia (1955–1958), while a new wharf and other facilities were completed in Port aux Basques. By the early 1960s, construction of the Newfoundland portion of the Trans-Canada Highway was well under way. With its completion in 1965, the amount of vehicle traffic to and from Newfoundland doubled almost overnight. The *William Carson* was finally able to fulfil its destiny as the first of a new generation of super-ships.

By the mid-1970s, however, it had been replaced on the Gulf service by newer, more fuel- efficient ferries. The *William Carson* was reassigned to the seasonal Labrador service to Goose Bay, which usually ran from June to late November. As the first automobile ferry to run between Newfoundland and Labrador, it provided a level of service that had never been available before.

Unfortunately, the *William Carson* did not have long to serve on the Labrador run—less than three years to be exact. On the night of June 2, 1977, in an icefield off the coast of southern Labrador, it started to take on water and sank a few hours later. There was no wind and sea conditions were calm, so the 128 passengers and crew on board were able to abandon ship and were rescued the next morning after spending the night in lifeboats, or on ice floes. Lost with the ship were 1100 tons of general cargo, fifty cars and trucks, and over four thousand cases of beer for the Canadian and American military bases in Goose Bay!

SS *ELAINE* WITH THE VOOGHT BUILDING IN THE BACKGROUND, 1906

When the first settlers came to Cape Breton, the land was covered by thick forest, right down to the water's edge. The use of water for local travel, at first by canoe or small personal boats, therefore, was essential. By the mid-nineteenth century, however, regular scheduled public transportation was available on the island's waterways, especially the Bras D'Or Lakes. This type of service continued until the outbreak of World War Two in 1939. At this time, improved highways, trucks, and railways, made transport by boat redundant. The *Elaine*, owned by the Bras D'Or Navigation Company, provided a regular North Sydney—Bras D'Or Lakes service from about 1890 to the outbreak of World War One in 1914.

SS *MARION*—HARRINGTON'S WHARF, SYDNEY, 1910

The SS *Marion* was a side-wheeler, purchased by the Bras D'Or Steamship company in 1882. It was built in New York State and had originally served as an excursion boat on the Hudson River. When it came to Cape Breton, it was refitted with staterooms and new furniture and sailed between Sydney and Mulgrave on the mainland.

By 1910, the *Marion* was offering a tri-weekly service between Sydney Harbour and the Bras D'Or Lakes. Leaving Sydney early in the morning, it called at North Sydney, Big Bras D'Or, New Campbellton, Boulardarie Centre, Ross's Ferry, Big Harbour, Baddeck, Nyanza, and finally Whycocomagh, where it spent the night. With its large saloon, dining room, and spacious staterooms, it was the finest of all the freight and passenger boats that ran on the Bras D'Or Lakes in the early years of the twentieth century. The *Marion* was destroyed by fire on October 21, 1922, while at the wharf in Whycocomagh.

SS *PEERLESS*, c.1910

Built in 1886 specifically for the Cape Breton Electric Company, the steamship *Peerless* served on the Sydney–North Sydney run for forty-six years! On weekdays it made fourteen round-trips, with only five on Sundays. Certain trips, if the tides cooperated, also called at Point Edward and Westmount. It made its last crossing in 1932, after regular bus service was instituted between the two locations. The Sydney Hotel can be seen in the background as well as the new Masonic Hall, with its circular dome.

SS *PEERLESS*, 1948

In this evocative photo by Nelson Rice, the *Peerless* suffers a humiliating end to its forty-six year career (1886–1932) as a North Sydney—Sydney passenger ferry. It had been tied up at a wharf on the Esplanade in Sydney, where it sank following a bad winter storm.

THE *PAWNEE* ARRIVES, C.1915

An excellent photograph of the ferry *Pawnee* at the wharf of the Cape Breton Electric Company in North Sydney. The *Pawnee* was the first ferry operated by the company and entered service in 1901. It offered an hourly service, beginning at 6:30 A.M. between Sydney and North Sydney, with frequent side trips to Whitney Pier and Point Edward. The large number of well-dressed passengers on board suggest a harbour cruise or some sort of holiday celebration. Judging by the flag on its stern, the large vessel behind it is a French battle cruiser, probably on a stopover to obtain "bunker coal" for its steam engines. Notice the cast-iron hot-water radiators on the wharf in the foreground.

***Aspy I*, the First Aspy Ferry , c.1920**

Built in 1912 for the North Shore Steamship Company in Sydney, the *Aspy I* made two sailings a week to northern Cape Breton. Leaving North Sydney, it would stop at St. Ann's, Englishtown, Breton Cove, North River, Ingonish, Neil's Harbour, Dingwall, and Bay St. Lawrence. It sank in a vicious September gale in 1924, off White Point in Aspy Bay. The eleven crew members and thirty-eight passengers all made it safely to shore in lifeboats.

At that time, when roads to northern Cape Breton were virtually non-existent, these communities were the Cape Breton equivalent of Newfoundland outports. They were isolated, and the only way in or out was by boat. When the spring pack ice arrived, they were often cut off from the outside world for three or four months. Therefore, the twice-weekly visit of the *Aspy* boats was an event eagerly awaited by the entire community. Freight, passengers, livestock, and the Royal Mail all arrived on these "steamers," along with the latest newspapers and magazines.

***Aspy II*, 1927**

This ship was built in 1925 for the North Shore Steamship Company. It was the second of three ships to bear the same name, and all operated on a regular basis from North Sydney to northern Cape Breton. This ship ran until the end of World War Two, while the third *Aspy* ran from 1946 to the mid-1950s. By then, improved highways had made the "Down North Ferries" unnecessary.

A DERELICT *ASPY II*, C.1950

Tied up and left to rot near the Ballast Grounds in North Sydney, this decrepit-looking vessel was once the pride of the "Down North" ferry service. The still-intact windows of the wheelhouse stand as mute witnesses to the many voyages that this ship made over a span of twenty years.

First Railway Station, c.1900

Under the terms of Confederation, in 1867, the new Canadian Government established the Intercolonial Railway to link the Maritime Provinces to Quebec and Ontario. However, it was not until 1885 that surveys for the new Cape Breton railroad were completed. The route would run from Port Hastings on the Strait of Canso to Georges River (Scotch Lake), and then on to Sydney. Needless to say, the mayor and town council of North Sydney were not too pleased with this arrangement, which also bypassed Florence, Bras D'Or, and Sydney Mines.

Thanks to political pressure exerted by the residents of the north-side, a branch line was completed in 1892, from the railway station at Scotch Lake, known as "The Junction", to North Sydney. The North Sydney "Branch" followed the north shore of Pottle's Lake into the town of North Sydney, passing through the present site of the North Sydney Mall on its way to the Newfoundland ferry wharf. The "Sydney Branch" went from Scotch Lake around the southern end of Pottle's Lake, and on to Leitches Creek and Sydney.

By 1914 both of these "Branch" lines were shut down and the tracks removed. The new rail line followed the shore of the Bras D'Or lakes, from George's River to Little Bras D'Or, Florence, Sydney Mines, North Sydney and on to Sydney. The original "Branch" line from Scotch Lake into North Sydney was recently upgraded and is now part of the Trans-Canada Trail.

This rather ornate train station, with second-floor living quarters for the station master, was completed in 1892. In 1928, this building was sold to John C. MacMillan, who jacked it up and moved it several hundred feet along Station Street to the site of MacMillan's Lumber Yard. A new, smaller station was built on the old site.

North Sydney Railway Station, 1929

The 7 P.M. express train arrives in Sydney from Halifax. The tracks draw your eye into the centre of the photograph, where the massive bulk of the steam engine completely dominates the scene. On the right, behind the 1929 Reo Flying Cloud automobile, is the "local" freight shed, where freight for the town was held until distributed. Behind the freight shed is the station itself, with a freight cart on the station platform. There was a separate, much larger, Newfoundland freight shed, where freight for that "overseas colony" was stored until ready to be shipped across the Cabot Strait by boat.

Queen Street, Sunday Afternoon Ride, 1902

The inscription on the back of this charming photograph states: "Happy party out for a drive in horse and buggies rented from Cogan's Livery Stable. In front of Crowell's place, 1902." Before the age of the automobile, this was a common way for families or groups of friends to spend a Sunday afternoon. Notice the brand-new electric streetcar (tramcar) tracks that ran from Kelly's Beach along the waterfront to Sydney Mines. The tramcar service started in 1901.

FACE TO FACE, c.1920

A white mare, hitched to a freight wagon, stares down a 1919 Buick Roadster on Commercial Street. Charles Ballard, from Sydney Mines, is the driver of this early convertible, while "Gil" Willis handles the reins of the horse. The building behind, with Neil Young's Tailor Shop on the left, no longer exists. Today this site is the entrance to the Ballast Grounds.

CHEVROLET TOURING SEDAN, 1915

The first Owl Drug Store opened in 1915, on the west corner of Commercial and Caledonia Streets. It was owned by Fraser Colquhoun and destroyed by fire in 1945. The owner then moved the business to the north corner of Commercial and King Streets, where it continued to operate until just a few years ago.

STAN CLEARY TAXI, 1947 PONTIAC STREAMLINER

This brand-new car cost $1850 (approximately $16,000 today). It produced 103 horsepower from a six-cylinder engine and weighed about two tons! Pontiac and Dodge vehicles were considered more upscale than their lower priced Ford, Chevrolet, and Plymouth contemporaries. This Pontiac was one of the first civilian cars produced in Canada after World War Two. It was virtually impossible to buy a new car during the war because the automobile factories had been converted to produce tanks, jeeps, and heavy-duty trucks for the Canadian Armed Forces. An interesting footnote: It was only in 1946 that a Canadian-built Chevrolet became the first vehicle to travel across Canada, from Halifax to Vancouver, using only Canadian highways!

Chapter 4

North Sydney and the Military

Off to the Boer War, 1899

North-side members of the Cape Breton Highlanders pose before shipping out for active duty in the Boer War in South Africa. This small-scale conflict between new British settlers in South Africa and the descendants of the original Dutch settlers (Boers), lasted for three years (1899– 1901). With the help of soldiers from Canada and other British colonies, the Boer resistance collapsed, and England succeeded in holding onto this important colonial outpost.

INDIAN BEACH (NORTH BAR), CURTISS FLYING BOATS, 1917

Shortly after the United States declared war on Germany on April 6, 1917, arrangements were made with the Canadian Government to station a squadron of four American flying boats (seaplanes) at North Sydney, to provide anti-submarine air patrols for convoys leaving Sydney Harbour for the war in Europe. More than two hundred American servicemen came by train, while the flying boats arrived in crates by boat.

While permanent quarters were under construction at Kelly's Beach, the American men and machines were stationed at Indian Beach. The men lived in tents, and wooden runways and ramps were built for the planes when they came out of the water. The planes would land in the water, run up on floating cradles, and these cradles would than be towed up onto shore. The process was reversed when they wanted to take off.

In this panoramic view taken from Purves Street, two flying boats are seen in the water, while a third rests on the wooden runway on the beach. The sandbar at South Bar, on the other side of the harbour, is just visible as a thin line between the two boats on the left.

Indian Beach, Curtiss Flying Boat, White Tents, and American Officers, 1917

Glenn Curtiss was a young American from New York State who built bicycles and motorcycles, and had a leading role in the development of the American aviation industry. He was a founding member of the Aerial Experiment Association, set up by Alexander Graham Bell, which designed and built several primitive airplanes. The most famous was "The Silver Dart," which flew from the frozen surface of Baddeck Bay on February 23, 1909, the first airplane flight in Canada and the British Empire. Curtiss later went on to design and build seaplanes, or flying boats as they were originally called, and four of his aircraft were stationed in North Sydney.

Kelly's Beach Barracks Across from Munro Park, 1917

By early 1917, a military base was under construction on both sides of the highway. It would house two hundred American and two hundred Canadian servicemen, along with dining facilities (mess halls), recreation areas, storage buildings, and a large seaplane hangar. Used in both world wars, most of the buildings, including the hangar, were dismantled by the late 1950s. However, four of these military buildings still exist today, one on the water side, and three on the hill by Musgrave Lane.

STUBBERT'S POINT BATTERY, C.1945

This coastal artillery emplacement, located in Centerville, contained two six-pounder Hotchkiss guns, an observation tower, and three large General Electric searchlights located in concrete bunkers built into the cliffs. Mounted on a movable carriage, these massive lights were five feet in diameter, produced eight hundred million candlepower, and could illuminate a ship up to five miles away. Needless to say, the residents of South Bar and vicinity, on the other side of the harbour, were none too pleased when their premises were illuminated at all hours of the night by these powerful searchlight beams! The concrete emplacements of this battery are still in place and can be seen on the shore road to Sydney Mines.

Anti-submarine Net and Buoys, 1945

Although taken at the entrance to Halifax Harbour, this picture gives a good idea of the type of anti-submarine net that extended from Stubbert's Point across the harbour entrance to South Bar. The net was made up of large steel cables, attached to floats on the surface, and concrete anchors on the harbour bottom. There was a "gate" in the middle of the net that could be opened to allow friendly vessels to enter the harbour. All ships arriving at the harbour entrance after dark would have to stop and be checked by the searchlights at Stubbert's Point. If they were friendly, the "gate" in the submarine net would be opened, and the ship could then enter the inner harbour. If the ships turned out to be enemy vessels, then the guns of Stubbert and other batteries around the harbour would open fire.

Convoy, Anti-Submarine Net, and Gate Vessel in the North Sydney Harbour, c.1944

A fascinating low-level aerial photograph taken from a military seaplane based at Kelly's Beach. Approximately forty ships, large and small, are waiting to join a convoy and head across the dangerous waters of the North Atlantic to the British Isles. In the lower foreground are the surface floats from which the steel cables of the anti-submarine net were suspended. This net extended all the way to the harbour bottom. At this point in the harbour the water depth ranges from twenty-four feet, near shore, to fifty-two feet in the centre channel. Also visible is the small ship that opened and closed the "gate," which would allow ships to enter or leave the safety of the inner harbour.

Convoy Waiting to Sail, Sydney Harbour, 1940

A striking close-up image, taken from an altitude of three hundred feet, looking towards South Bar. These thirty-nine ships were part of a larger convoy that sailed from Sydney on November 7, 1940. Convoys that sailed in the late fall, or during the winter months would often fall prey to treacherous storms and ice conditions, as well as the ever present danger of enemy submarines.

Slow Convoy (SC-41), August 24, 1941

"SC" also stood for "Sydney, Nova Scotia, to the river Clyde (Glasgow) in Scotland."

In this remarkable photograph, taken by a Royal Canadian Air Force flying boat stationed at Kelly's Beach in North Sydney, thirty-seven (out of forty-three) fully-laden merchant ships head for the west coast of Newfoundland on their way to the British Isles.

Because the normal route along the south coast of Newfoundland was so dangerous, it was decided to send this convoy through the Strait of Belle Isle, between northern Newfoundland and Labrador. They would then travel past Greenland and Iceland and around the northern tip of Ireland. However, a combination of heavy fog and bad ice conditions resulted in serious damage to six ships, due to collisions with icebergs. All six were able to return to Sydney.

In the left background you can see northern Cape Breton and Cape North.

***Canso* Flying Boat, c.1944**

The aerial pictures of Sydney Harbour and various convoys in this book were taken by this type of seaplane, flying from the naval air station at Kelly's Beach (Munro Park). These Royal Canadian Air Force seaplanes were known as "amphibians." They could land on water or, by means of retractable landing gear, on a normal airport runway. Designed for long range anti-submarine patrol, the *Canso* was also used for search and rescue operations. Thanks to its ability to land on the ocean, it was able to rescue many survivors of torpedo attacks against Allied convoys. (In one eight-month period, between May and November 1942, eighteen ships were sunk by German submarines in either the Gulf of St. Lawrence or the Cabot Strait!)

First produced in the United States in 1933, a total of more than thirty-four hundred seaplanes were built, including eight hundred manufactured in Canada during World War Two. The most popular flying boat in history, it was used by the armed forces of Canada, Britain, Australia, Russia, and the United States. The *Canso* was sixty-three feet long and had a wing span of 104 feet. With a top speed of 175 mph, and a range of twenty-three hundred miles, it was armed with five machine guns and could carry two tons (four thousand pounds) of bombs or depth charges. It carried a crew of seven. Notice the observation "blisters" on the rear fuselage. These were used for patrol work, and could be opened to allow machine guns to be used against enemy fighter aircraft.

Final Visit Home, Five Siblings, 1942

Left to right: Donnie MacLean; Sergeant Rannie MacLean; Hector MacLean (father); Pat MacLean; George MacLean; Mary (MacLean) Gillis.

On his final home leave before being shipped overseas, Sergeant Rannie MacLean proudly wears his flying tunic, with "Navigator/Observer Wing" on his left breast. While a student at St. Francis Xavier University in Antigonish, Rannie had won medals for intercollegiate boxing. He never returned from his seventh anti-submarine mission off the coast of France.

Donnie and George MacLean tried to join the Canadian Army but were turned down, because their jobs were considered vital to the war effort on the home front. Donnie was a telegrapher with Canadian National Railways, and George was a carpenter at the naval base in Sydney. Their brother Pat was a student at St. F. X. University, while Mary was married and expecting her first child.

Mary, and many other women in North Sydney, volunteered their time as members of the local Red Cross Society. They would meet several afternoons each week, to knit heavy woolen socks, caps, scarves, and sweaters for the troops overseas. When not knitting, they would often prepare small packages of food, candy, cigarettes, and persona items like soap and toothpaste. These "Care Packages" would then be sent through the International Red Cross Society to allied troops in prisoner of war camps in occupied Europe. Rannie MacLean was one of 68 men from North Sydney who lost their lives in the Second World War. The small town lost sixty-six men in the First World War!

Margaret Nicholson and American soldiers, c.1917

Margaret Nicholson on the steps of her family home at 77 Archibald Avenue. The two soldiers with her were among the two hundred United States military personnel stationed at the naval air station at Kelly's Beach (Munro Park) from 1917– 1919. Less than one year after this picture was taken, Maggie died of the Spanish Flu at the young age of eighteen. The Spanish flu killed twenty-one million people worldwide between 1918–1919, including some fifty thousand Canadians. It was brought back to Canada by troops returning from World War One in Europe and made its way into the remotest communities. A number of villages in Quebec and Labrador were almost totally exterminated by the disease. It got its name because it allegedly killed eight million people in Spain, in one month!

Burning Liberty Ship, 1943

In August, 1943, the United States freighter SS *J. Pinkerton Henderson* collided with another ship in convoy off the south coast of Newfoundland. Although the hull was not badly damaged, a serious fire broke out in barrels of oil carried on deck. Soon, another blaze was raging below decks, in cargo holds full of lumber, cotton, ammunition, and magnesium ingots. This fire resulted in several explosions and the release of poisonous gasses which quickly killed sixty-four of the sixty-seven crew members.

Still on fire six days later, the ship was towed to Cape Breton, where a local harbour pilot named Milton MacKenzie boarded the ship outside the anti-submarine net and supervised its entry into North Sydney Harbour. It took twenty-four days for naval fire-fighting crews from Sydney and Halifax to extinguish the fires! Of the sixty-four crew members who perished, only thirty-two bodies were recovered. These remains were buried in a mass grave in the Hardwood Hill Cemetery in Sydney. At the end of the war, the remains were exhumed and returned to the United States for burial.

For his courage and bravery in a very dangerous situation, Captain Milton MacKenzie received the MBE (Member of the British Empire). The MBE was one of the top awards for heroism in wartime awarded in the former British Empire.

New Legion Hall, 1948

The first Royal Canadian Legion meeting in North Sydney took place in 1927, on an upper floor of the old town hall. In 1940, a "War Service Hut" was established on Archibald Avenue at the site of the present Legion Hall. At the end of World War Two in 1945, this building from the former naval air station at Kelly's Beach was purchased by the local branch and moved to Archibald Avenue. It was enlarged to its present size in 1968.

Armstrong Memorial, Branch 19, has remained one of the most active Royal Canadian Legion groups in the province of Nova Scotia. In addition to many community activities, it has been the guiding light behind the operation and success of 562 Cabot Squadron of the Royal Canadian Air Cadets. During Canada's Centennial Celebrations in 1967, this squadron was named the top Air Cadet squadron in Canada!

Chapter 5

Public Services:
Schools, Churches, and Hospital

St. Joseph's Catholic Church Complex, c.1897

This rare picture gives an excellent view of the "Catholic Complex" that existed on the side of Goat Hill in Ward Four. The first Catholic Church was built about 1844, on the location of the former St. Joseph's Convent. The graveyard in the centre of the picture was also in use at that time. The church in this picture was the second Catholic Church, built in 1883, at the same time as the Glebe House (Priest's House) on the top of the hill. In 1908 the Glebe House became the Hamilton Hospital. The large building on the left is St. Joseph's School.

There was a time around the turn of the last century when almost all the members of the Catholic community in North Sydney lived on the northern outskirts of this predominately Protestant town. This area contained the Catholic Church, the Catholic School, a Convent, and the Catholic burial ground. If you were born in that area, you could be baptised in the Church, obtain your education in the school, get married in the Church, have your funeral in the Church, and be buried in the graveyard, all within a radius of less than a hundred yards! The graveyard closed in 1912, except for family plots, when a new graveyard was opened on the Johnston Road.

THE SIDE OF GOAT HILL, 1976

This view, from the right hand side of the graveyard, shows the former Hamilton Hospital (later Stella Maris Seniors Residence) on the left, Mount St. Joseph Convent in the centre, and the Junior High School on the right.

Grade Four Boys, St. Joseph's Elementary School, 1942

The grade four boys class formed up in ranks on the school playground to hear a "pep talk" on the war effort from an unidentified soldier in the foreground. These events took place on a regular basis during the war years. In the background is the Junior High School, while Hamilton Memorial Hospital is on the top of the hill to the left.

St. Joseph's School Complex, 1976

This shot of the St. Joseph's School Complex was taken just months before it was torn down. Taken from the lower end of Convent Street, it shows a familiar scene that will bring back many memories to the thousands of students who attended these hallowed halls of learning. St. Joseph's High, where I taught social studies (1966–1976), is on the left. In the centre background is the elementary school, while the junior high is on the right.

The history of St. Joseph's School dates back to 1883, when four members of the Sisters of Charity arrived in Halifax and then made their way to North Sydney. We even know their names: Sister Mary Cleophas, Sister Maria Hurley, Sister Mary Vincentia Rose, and Sister Mary Regis Hoare were to form the nucleus of the many Sisters of Charity who followed their legacy down through the years.

The first classes were held in the basement of the second Catholic Church on Convent Street, which opened in 1883. In 1888, a new large school with eight classrooms was built on the side of Goat Hill adjacent to the new church. Only four of these rooms were used during the first few years. In 1913, a new junior high school was built on the original foundation of the second church, which had been destroyed by fire in 1907. The senior high school opened in 1925, which completed the triangle of education for St. Joseph's students.

St. Joseph's Elementary, 1976

After eighty-eight years, the first school in the complex (1888–1976) was starting to show its advanced age. Notice the state of the roof. When I attended this school back in the late 1940s and early 1950s, the eight classrooms were heated by pot-bellied stoves that required constant care. If your seat was close to the stove, you would be too hot. If you sat by the windows, you could be too cold, thanks to drafts of cold air. Students in the centre classrooms on the upper level who wished to go to the bathroom would have to make their way through adjoining classrooms on either side to reach the stairways at either end of the building. Conditions were primitive, to say the least, but we all learned to read, write, and do basic arithmetic!

Regent Street School, c.1905

Built in 1892 at a cost of four thousand dollars, this striking eight-room school was considered to be the finest on Cape Breton Island. In the early years it did not have electricity, and elementary classes would often be sent home early on dark winter afternoons. Junior and senior high students, however, had to soldier on as best they could. The school was destroyed by fire in 1947.

The four-room building on the left was the new high school, which opened in 1903 to relieve overcrowding in the original school building. At first it housed both junior and senior high school students, but the senior high classes left in 1936 for Central School on Stanley Street. The 1903 building was later known as Park Street Elementary School. It closed in 1974.

SECOND CATHOLIC CHURCH, WITH FLAGS, 1883

On September 16, 1883, the new St. Joseph's church on Convent Street was officially blessed, and the first mass was celebrated by Bishop John Cameron of Antigonish. Built in the Gothic style, it was considered one of the most beautiful churches in the province of Nova Scotia. It replaced the first small church, on the other side of the street, which had outlived its usefulness. Mount St. Joseph Convent (Sisters of Charity) is on the left.

Vooght Wedding at St. John's Anglican Church, 1906

The wedding of Thomas Vooght Jr. to Ethel Bertram was the social event of the season in 1906. Politicians, dignitaries, and the social elite of the northside were all part of this ostentatious occasion, as befitted the grandson of one of the owners of the largest department store east of Montreal!

Built on the corner of King and Pleasant Streets, with the front of the church facing the harbour, this was the third building to serve as a place of worship for this congregation. The first small church was built on the same location in 1877, and was enlarged in 1886 to accommodate a growing number of church members. However, within a few years, even this facility was too small, and it was moved to the rear of the lot facing King Street and used as a church hall. It was replaced, on the original site, by a new and impressive wooden building in 1903. This new structure lasted until January, 1959, when both it and the church hall were destroyed by fire. A new hall was quickly built, with an entrance on Pierce Street. This served as a temporary church until a brand-new, very modern-looking building was opened in 1966.

St. Matthew–Wesley United Church, c.1904

The first St. Matthew's Presbyterian Church of Canada was built on the corner of Queen and Peppett Streets in 1876, at a cost of approximately five thousand dollars. In 1898, this structure was moved back to form a hall, and a new church was built on the corner. One year later, a serious fire caused considerable damage to the building, and a third church was built on the same site in 1901. In 1925, when the Methodist and Presbyterian Churches of Canada came together to form the United Church of Canada, the two congregations in North Sydney decided to worship in this building. From then on it was known as St. Matthew–Wesley United Church.

The minister in the insert photo is Rev. Chalmers Jack, who was pastor from 1896 to 1918.

Calvary Baptist Church, c.1908

Members of the first formal church in town, this congregation can trace its beginnings back to 1825. After sharing a meeting place with another religious organization for a number of years, they decided to build their own church in Upper North Sydney. This building, which opened in 1846, was located next to the present-day MacCormick's Esso service station. Thirty years later, in 1876, they decided to move to town and built a new church on the corner of Park and Beech Streets. The present church, on the same site, was built in 1914.

St. Joseph's Catholic Church, Archibald Avenue, 1920

In 1907 the former St. Joseph's Church on Convent Street was destroyed by fire. Construction of a new church on the corner of Archibald Avenue and Pierce Street started in 1910. It took two years to build, and was officially opened on May 12, 1912. The new church, which seats one thousand people, was designed by the famous Maritime architect William Critchlow Harris (1854–1913).

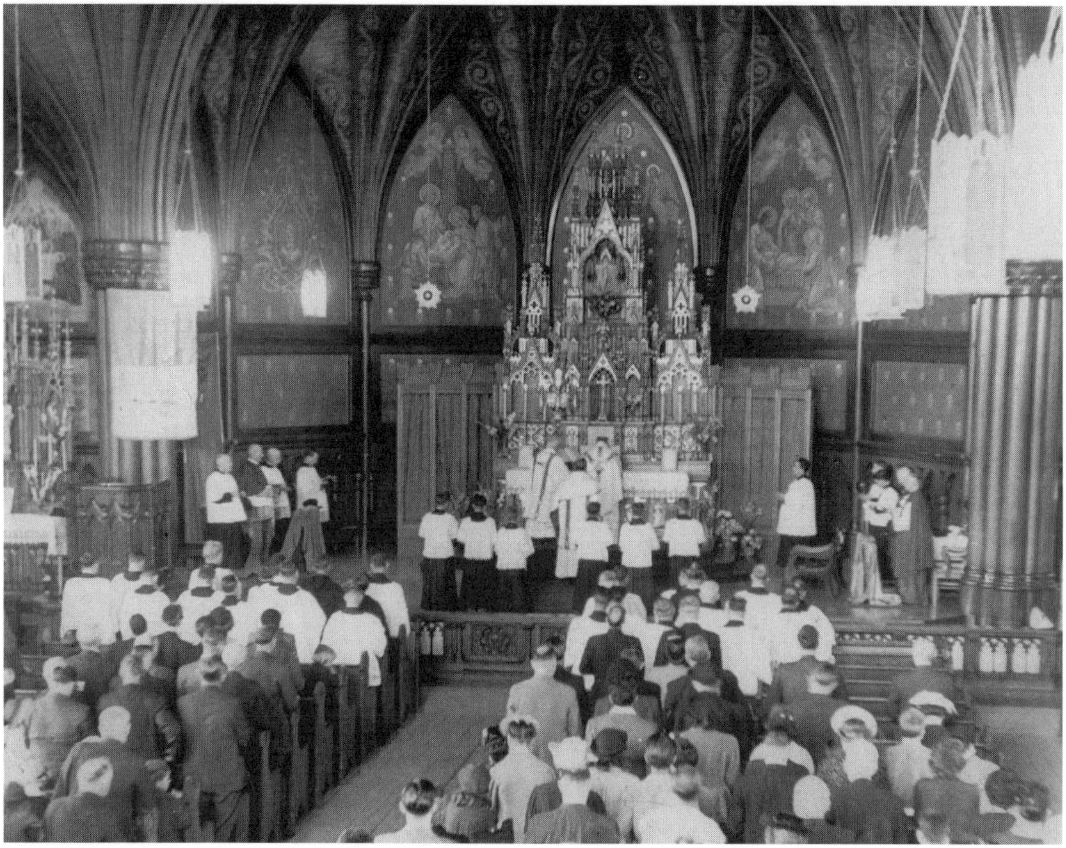

One Hundredth Anniversary of St. Joseph's Mission Church, 1946

On September 2, 1946, the parishoners of St. Joseph's gathered to celebrate the one hundredth anniversary of the first church of any denomination in North Sydney. Although the first Catholic Church was built in 1844, on Goat Hill near Convent Street, it was not until 1846 that it became an official "mission" church of the Sydney Parish. St. Joseph's did not become a separate parish until 1853.

PAINTING THE STEEPLE, C.1940

At 175 feet, the steeple of St. Joseph's Catholic Church is the highest steeple in the Diocese of Antigonish! These two unknown painters are using Bosun's Chairs, suspended from the top of the steeple, to apply the first of two coats of paint. Needless to say, this type of job was only undertaken when it was really necessary.

The First Choir of St. Joseph's Church, c.1907

The first "official" choir was formed in the early years of the twentieth century, and by the time of this photograph had achieved a certain degree of harmony and cohesion.

Front row, left to right: Josephine Tobin, Bernie Desmond, Kate Hartigan, Winnie Connors, Etta MacDermott;

Second row: Ed Gannon, Bessie (Connell) Murphy, Maggie (Gannon) Boissonoult, Richard Hickey, Bridget (Gannon) Brennan;

Third row: Mrs. Dr. R.C. MacLeod, Arcade Boissonoult, Mae MacPherson, Cecilia (Murphy) Hurley;

Back row: Nellie Musgrave, Mary Desmond, Bob Phalen, John Cogan, Neil MacMillan, Nell (Holland) Hickey.

St. Joseph's Choir, 1947

In the forty years since the formation of the first mixed choir in 1907, the reputation of this singing group had reached the point where it was standing room only for Solemn High Mass, in four-part harmony, on Christmas Eve and Easter Sunday. It was even reported that non-Catholic residents of the town were often in attendance at such musical events! Today, this tradition continues with the Senior Choir, Folk Choir, and Funeral Choir.

Front row, left to right: Hilda Robinson, Geraldine Walsh, Nora (Ryan) Tobin, Kal Ryan, Helen (Balah) Dunn (Director), Maude MacDonald, Nixie (MacNeil) Leger, Lydia (Herue) Smith;

Second row: Donnie MacLean, John Perry, Kay (Burns) MacEachern, Vivian Mancini, Aggie Andrea, Tommy Thorne;

Third row: Joe Whalen, Mary B. MacDonald, Marie Logue, Josie (Lamey) Abraham, Morrisey Dunn, George Thorne;

Fourth row: Mae Garab, Veronica Gillis;

Fifth row: Alfred Abraham, Dave Balah, Frank Whalen, Dave Thorne, Kilmer Dunn, Gerard Dunn, Tom (Tubby) MacDonald;

Back row (top left): Angus Beaton.

HAMILTON HOSPITAL, 1921

Built as a Glebe House for St. Joseph's Parish circa 1883, this building was bought by a Mr. Alexander Hamilton in 1908, who then gave it to the Sisters of Charity to use as North Sydney's first hospital. In 1930 a new maternity wing was added to the building, followed by another new section in 1940. When the new St. Elizabeth Hospital opened in 1954, the former Hamilton Hospital became a senior citizens' guest home, renamed as the Stella Maris (Star of the Sea) Residence.

Chapter 6

Sports, Leisure, and Entertainment

COASTING, UPPER ARCHIBALD AVENUE, 1945

A happy group of children take advantage of winter on the hill next to the home of Nora Tobin, 80 Archibald Avenue. With a suitable "spotter" at the railroad station to watch out for traffic, the sleighs and toboggans would often continue to coast down the "Station Hill" to the parking lot at the bottom!

BILLY HOOD, DRIVER, AT NORTHSIDE DOWNS (NORTH SYDNEY TROTTING PARK), 1935

When this half-mile-long racetrack opened on July 1, 1898, one year before a similar facility in Sydney, it was considered to be the fastest such track in the province. It was also the first time that rubber-tired sulkies were used in Cape Breton, as iron-wheeled carts were used previously. In the years before and after World War One, harness racing was very popular; tracks in Sydney, North Sydney, and Glace Bay all vied for the racing fan's dollar. By the early 1930s, however, the North Sydney track was so popular that it almost put the other two out of business. In 1936 the Cape Breton County Exhibition built a number of new buildings adjacent to the track, and harness racing became a regular feature of the annual exhibition. After a new racetrack was opened in Sydney in 1944, the North Sydney track was used only as a training facility.

St. Joseph's High School Baseball Team, 1949–1950

These eager young men prepare to take part in a local high-school tournament. Their borrowed uniforms came from the Sydney Mines Royals.

Batboy in front: Bud Devoe;

Front row, left to right: Joe Young, Aubrey Gouthro, Mickey Andrea, Kevin Steele, Ed Lawless, Donnie Steele;

Rear row: Father R. D. Smith, Ron (Bomber) Andrea, Artie Clark, Bud Day, John Edwards, John Coleman, teacher/coach Tom MacDonald.

Indian Beach, 1920

Officially known as "North Bar," this large sandbar had been used in early years as a summer encampment for the local Mi'kmaq community on the side of Ferris Hill. Indian Beach has remained the most popular swimming spot in North Sydney for more than two centuries. Goat Hill is in the background.

Diving Boards at Indian Beach, 1934

The wooden tower in the background contains three diving boards at different heights, as well as a water slide for the younger children.

YACHTING AT INDIAN BEACH, C.1934

Yacht races were held almost every weekend during the summer season, attracting boats from Sydney, Coxheath, and even Baddeck.

FIRST GAME AT NORTH SYDNEY FORUM, 1948

On January 12, 1948, the first game in the new North Sydney Forum was held between the Northside Victorias and the Glace Bay Miners (the Victorias won!). The building had been purchased after World War Two from a naval base in Digby County on the mainland. It was dismantled in sections and shipped to North Sydney on railroad flat-cars. The building had been used during World War Two as an aircraft hangar at a naval base in Deep Brook, Digby County.

Queen Hotel Hockey Team, 1910–1911

The Queen Hotel was located on Blowers Street, next to the present day Dooley's Billiard Parlour. It opened circa 1900, with rooms advertised for $2.50 a night. It was destroyed by fire in 1929.

Top row, left to right: D. Dooley, A. McFee, J. Ross;
Middle row: W. Wilkie, D. Butts, J.W. Anderson, J. McLean;
Bottom row: J. Batterson, A. McKinnon, G. Gannon.

Franklin Juniors, 1952–1953

This team, sponsored by the Franklin Coal Mine in Bras D'Or, played the Ottawa Porcupine Combines for the Memorial Cup. The game was played in the Northside Forum.

Front row, left to right: "Digger" MacDonald, Ron "Bomber" Andrea, unknown, Joe Collins, Jackie MacLeod, Vince Ryan, Ronnie Clark, Aubrey Gouthro;

Second row: Gerald Bartlett, Donnie Steele, Alvin Higgins, Cyril Doucette, Bernie Andrea, Peter MacIntosh, Bert Dalling, Teddy Andrea, Mickey Roach (Coach);

Third row: Willie Dunn, Billy Billick, Enver Sampson (Sec.-Treas.), Russ MacDonald (Manager), John Vallance (President), Eddie Kayes, "Dinky" Dorrington.

NATAL DAY PARADE, 1934

A large group of onlookers watches the parade approach the bottom of Archibald Avenue. Natal Day is a civic holiday celebrated in Nova Scotia on the first Monday in August. The steeple of St. Joseph's Catholic Church is in the background.

NORTH SYDNEY VICTORIAS 1922-1923

The Victorias hockey team, first organized in 1900, played many games against teams from Sydney, Sydney Mines, Glace Bay and New Waterford. They were Nova Scotia hockey champions in 1912–13.

Front row, left to right: Kenneth McKenzie, R. Gordon;

Middle row: H. McLean, P. Bill, J. Barrington, L. Fowler, N. MacMillan;

Back row: L. Cossman, B. Wheller, B. MacDonald, D. Watson, C. Ingraham, J. McKenzie.

NORTH SYDNEY (NORTHSIDE) VICTORIAS, 1947–1948

Members of the Cape Breton Senior Hockey League, the Victorias of 1947–48 had a former National Hockey League star on their roster as a player and coach. Gordie Drillon, from Moncton, New Brunswick, had a brief but remarkable career in the National Hockey League. As a member of the Toronto Maple Leafs, he won the scoring title and Lady Byng Trophy in 1938–39, and the Stanley Cup in 1942. He was later traded to the Montreal Canadiens, but left professional hockey in 1943 to join the Canadian Army. At the end of the war he returned to the Maritimes, where he played senior hockey with various teams. He became a member of the Hockey Hall of Fame in 1975.

Front Row, left to right: W. Sheperd, M. Bentley, C. Dowling, T. Tomori, B. Stanton, H. Rosseau, R. Carver; Bobby O'Neill in front with towel;

Back Row: G. Drillon (coach), B. Verrier, S. DeQuoi;,G. Gallipeau, M. Strahan, S. Milne, J. Curtiss, W. Shurget, H. Carrington (trainer).

Ski Chalet at Ferris Hill, 1934

This rough log cabin, with hot tea and fresh coffee, was built during the height of the Great Depression (1929–1939). In an age before unemployment insurance, this construction project, including the ski slope and toboggan run on the side of the hill, was a "make-work" project for local unemployed men. It was also rumored that various forms of alcoholic beverages were available, for medicinal reasons only!

Ski Slope and Toboggan Run at Ferris Hill, 1934

This was the only public ski slope in the province of Nova Scotia, while the toboggan run was considered to the best of its kind east of Montreal. Lights on poles illuminated the scene at night. With the outbreak of World War Two in 1939, the complex was shut down.

North Sydney Hawks, 1937

Three members of a junior hockey team pose. In 1937, team members decided to build their own full-size outdoor rink (Hawks' Arena), on the corner of Stanley and Forman Streets. They cut their own lumber in the woods, had it processed at MacMillan's Lumber Yard, and hooked up a system of lights for night-time use. This successful rink was also used for skating parties and other social events. It continued in seasonal operation until the Northside Forum opened in 1948.

Left to right: Normie Jesty, Gordie Logan, and George MacLean.

EMPIRE HALL GYM CLASS, c.1918

Built in 1901 by St. Joseph's Parish, the Empire Hall was located at the lower end of Blowers Street, where Dooley's Billiard Parlour is today. For the next fifty years, this two-storey building served as a focal point for local concerts, plays, minstrel shows, and other social events. The gym was located on the ground floor and was the site of many dances and fancy dress balls. During World War Two, the Empire Hall served as a Knights of Columbus hostel and was often used to provide temporary accommodation and recreation for the many servicemen and women who passed through the town. It was destroyed by fire in 1950.

NORTHERN YACHT CLUB AND KELLY'S BEACH, C.1950

The Northern Yacht Club was organized in 1924, near Indian Beach. Its first clubhouse is now Rollie's Wharf Restaurant and Bar. In 1948 the Club moved to its present location near Kelly's Beach, because of increased ship traffic in the inner harbour and problems with coal dust from the coal-shipping piers.

Chapter 7

People

TRAIN STATION, 1945

A charming picture of Russell MacDonald and his daughter Arlene, with her brand-new sleigh. A native of Port Morien, Russell worked underground for many years at the Franklin Coal Mine in Bras D'Or. In the early 1960s he became caretaker at St. Joseph's Parish Centre in North Sydney and later worked as a bartender at the Seaview Curling and Golf Club in Upper North Sydney. Arlene, who later worked in the port office at the Newfoundland Ferry Terminal, retired in 1990 after thirty-four years with Marine Atlantic.

Dr. L. R. (Lloyd) Meech, 1948

Dr. Meech (1893–1968), a native of Sydney, served with the famous Black Watch Highland Regiment of the British Army during World War One, receiving the Military Cross. He opened his medical practice in North Sydney in 1921 and for the next forty-four years was a mainstay of the medical profession on the north-side. He became well-known, far and wide, for his house calls at any time of the day or night, and in various types of inclement weather. When he "officially" retired in 1965, he was honoured by his peers and the town for an incredible fifty years of service in the medical field.

During World War Two, following in their father's footsteps, three of Dr. Meech's sons joined the Canadian Armed Forces. He and his wife (Mary Josephine) would later suffer a personal tragedy when two of their sons, Lloyd and William, were killed in action.

DR. J. S. (JEPTHA SETH) MUNRO, 1948

A native of Belle Cote, Inverness County, Dr. Munro graduated from Dalhousie Medical School in 1919. For the next eight years he practiced in Whycocomagh, Margaree, and Cape North, before moving to North Sydney in 1927. He had a medical practice in town for the better part of forty-eight years, until 1975. When he retired, he received many awards for his grand total of fifty-six years in the medical profession! He served as mayor of North Sydney for sixteen consecutive years, from 1957 to 1973. As part of Canada's centennial celebrations in 1967, a recreational complex at Kelly's Beach was renamed as Munro Park, in honour of the man who had devoted so many years of his life to the well-being and prosperity of the town.

DISCUSSING TOWN AFFAIRS, 1947

In the warmer months, after the long winter and cold, damp spring, many of the older retired men in town would meet on a regular basis at one of several locations along the waterfront. At these informal gatherings they would discuss local politics, town affairs, and the comings and goings of various individuals within the town.

In this charming Nelson Rice photograph, ten of North Sydney's citizens enjoy some summer sunshine in front of the town's fire station.

Left to right: Constable Jim Meaney, Gerald Cleary, R. Fougere, Constable Joe Hickey, Bart Edwards, Solicitor Reg MacNeil, M. Gouthro, Fred Musgrave, Police Chief Louis Clarke,Tom Lamie.

Walter Rice Fishing, c.1944

Born in 1878 in Little Bras D'Or, Walter Rice opened a women's and children's clothing store in North Sydney in the early years of the twentieth century. Located where the Nickerson office building now stands, this shop was destroyed in the great fire of 1913. Rice rebuilt, moving to the other side of Commercial Street. He later sold his business to Ted Bond, who in turn sold it to George Swan in 1964.

In his early years, Walter Rice was considered one of the top tennis players in the Maritime Provinces, if not eastern Canada. In 1916, at the age of thirty-eight, he won the Nova Scotia Men's Tennis Championship. For three straight years (1919, 1920, and 1921), he won the Maritime Singles Championship. On one occasion, he was invited by the Canadian Lawn Tennis Association to try out for Canada's Davis Cup Team, the tennis equivalent of the World Series or the Stanley Cup! He died in 1974, at the age of ninety-six.

Nelson Rice, c.1965

Born in Sydney Mines in 1906, Nelson and his family moved to North Sydney when he was twelve years old. After studies in Pharmacy at Dalhousie University in Halifax, he spent most of his working career at McCallum's Drug Store (later Rexall Drugs) on Commercial Street, followed by a few years at Capital Drugs in Sydney Mines. On his retirement he received a special certificate from the Pharmaceutical Society of Nova Scotia in recognition of his sixty-eight years in the profession. He died in 1994, at the age of eighty-eight. From his father Walter and grandfather Abner Rice, he inherited a life-long love of black and white photography. His home, on the corner of Archibald Avenue and Stanley Streets, contained its own darkroom, which was off-limits to family members. Here he painstakingly developed his negatives and printed his own photographs. He was never a commercial photographer, and his pictures were not for sale. However, if he took your picture, you would soon receive a suitable enlargement, and often more than one.

Over the years Nelson Rice developed a well-deserved reputation among his peers as a master photographer, and several of his photographs won national and international awards. However, in North Sydney he is best remembered for his many eloquent and lifelike portraits of his fellow townspeople, black and white photographs that rank as consummate examples of the photographer's art.

John Trenchard, Blacksmith, c.1948

A striking portrait by Nelson Rice of a man who spent his entire working life in the hot and dangerous confines of a blacksmith's shop. Taken outside of the blacksmith's forge, this beautiful character study captures the wisdom and maturity of the skilled tradesman's old age. Even in John Trenchard's advanced years, there is still a mischievous twinkle in his eyes!

Tom MacDonald, Blacksmith, c.1948

Nelson Rice took this picture of Tom MacDonald (1880–1963) at his forge on Prince Street. A native of Northeast Margaree, Tom set up his first shop near the Newfoundland ferry terminus. However, he was forced to give up his location when the Newfoundland service expanded during World War Two. He retired in 1950, at the age of seventy, when his forge was destroyed by fire.

Little John MacKinnon, c.1948.

Another classic Nelson Rice photo, taken by natural light at a window in the town's fire hall. "Little John" stood only five feet four inches tall, but was regarded as one of the best painters in the town of North Sydney. Exterior, interior, or individual piece work, Little John could do it all. A bachelor, he lived with his brother Joe MacKinnon, on the corner of Blowers and Pierce streets.

On a Honeymoon, July 10, 1941

When Albert Shebib and Alexandra Kawaja planned their marriage early in 1941, we can safely assume that the older members of their respective families had no idea that they would head out for their honeymoon on a motorcycle! Their 1941 Indian Scout was equipped with a large windshield, leather saddlebags, and white-sidewall tires with a suitcase strapped on top of the rear fender.

In what was undoubtedly a first for the north-side area, and probably Cape Breton Island, the smartly-dressed couple set out from the Shebib family home at 47 Archibald Avenue for an open-road adventure. The bride wore a two-piece pant suit with a white blouse, while the groom sported dress pants and a leather jacket. The groom's hands and forearms were protected by gauntlets, stout leather gloves with wide, flaring cuffs, and both wore soft leather motorcycle helmets. Aviator-style goggles protected their eyes from the wind, and the dust and debris thrown up from the dirt roads.

FIRE STATION GOSSIP AND FIRE TRUCK, 1945

The first primitive fire station in town was built in 1873, at the foot of Archibald Avenue, on the water side. A new, larger building was opened in 1913, at the lower end of Court Street. This was in use until 1932, when the department moved into this building at the foot of Archibald Avenue, close to the original site. The latest fire station was built at the lower end of Pierce Street in 1971.

Left to right: Bill Vardy, Constable Joe Hickey, Billy Parsons, unknown, Tom Roach.

V. E. (Victory in Europe) Day , May 5, 1945

Fourteen residents of North Sydney pose in front of the Rexall Drug Store on Commercial Street while celebrating the end of World War Two in Europe. (Japan had yet to be defeated.)

Left to right: Neil McInnes, Georgie (McLean) Coleman, Shirley (McLean) Murray, Stan Cleary, Jack Fraser, M. Phalen, Joe Whalen, Charles Coleman, Doug Matheson, Frank Collins, Harry Ivey, M. Fortune, Abe Astephen, Dan MacLeod.

VOLUNTEER FIRE DEPARTMENT, 1945

Bundled up against the intense cold, volunteer members of the town's fire department pose with Fire Chief William Parsons after an early morning fire in December, 1945. This picture was taken at the corner of Archibald Avenue and Commercial Street, with the Vooght Building in the background.

On another cold December morning, in 1881, the core of North Sydney's business district was destroyed by fire. Almost every building from Archibald Avenue to Caledonia Street, on both sides of the street, was lost. This was a particularly devastating fire since several warehouses containing most of the town's winter supplies were destroyed. There was no railroad at that time, so these supplies arrived each fall by ship. With the help of the good citizens of Sydney and Sydney Mines, the town was able to make it through the winter months until shipping resumed in late spring.

Another catastrophic fire took place in May, 1913, when forty-one business establishments were destroyed. This conflagration wiped out the same area as the 1881 blaze, as well as other assorted stores and shops. These included the Vooght Brothers' two warehouses and three warehouses belonging to J. W. Ingraham's General Store. Three years later, in 1916, the Nova Scotia Legislature sent a directive to the town of North Sydney stating that all new commercial buildings erected on either side of Commercial Street would have to be built of concrete, stone, or brick.

Left to right: Tom Lamie, Joe Reid, Chief Parsons, Fred Trenchard, and Nelson Hare.

Police Chief Louis Clark, 1935

In 1910, the Nova Scotia Temperance Act came into effect, banning the sale of all alcoholic beverages in the province, except those used for medicinal or religious purposes. Needless to say, this edict did not go down well in a seaport town like North Sydney, and a flourishing illicit liquor trade with the French islands of St. Pierre and Miquelon soon developed. Rum, scotch, and various grades of wine and liquors were soon available in selected "holes-in-the-wall" around town. They were also exported by rail and boat to all parts of the Maritime provinces and the east coast of the United States. It was the birth of the infamous "rum-runners"!

After 1917, when Prohibition came into force across Canada, the federal government hired many inspectors in a futile attempt to control this forbidden enterprise. Because of North Sydney's preeminent position as a leading port and its close proximity to St. Pierre and Miquelon, seven inspectors were assigned to the town. Although they were kept busy, the flow of contraband liquor continued unabated.

Louie Clarke was one of these inspectors. However, with the repeal of Prohibition in both Canada and the United States in 1933, their jobs became redundant. Louie then became Police Chief in North Sydney, a position he would hold for the next twenty-one years.

PROFESSIONAL GOOD FRIENDS, 1953

Left to right: Judge Murray (Ricky) Ryan; Senator John M. MacDonald; Dr. Bill Buchanan.

Ricky Ryan graduated from St. Joseph's High (Grade 11) and Sydney Mines High School (Grade 12), and took a Bachelor of Arts degree from St. Francis Xavier University in Antigonish. During World War Two, he spent two years with the Royal Canadian Navy, serving on corvettes escorting convoys in the North Atlantic Ocean. After the war, Ricky attended Dalhousie Law School in Halifax for three years. Following graduation in 1948 he practiced law in North Sydney for thirty-two years until he was appointed County Court Judge in 1982. He retired as a Supreme Court judge in 1994.

John M. MacDonald was a former dean of the Canadian senate and the last senator appointed for life. He came to the upper chamber in 1960 after a varied career as a teacher, lawyer, soldier and administrator. He died in 1997 at the age of 91.

Dr. Bill Buchanan was born in North Sydney in 1897. After graduating from high school, he attended the University of Maryland in Baltimore, receiving his Doctor of Dental Science in 1902. He practiced dentistry in town for the next forty-six years, until his death in 1966. He also served one four-year term as a Liberal Member of Parliament from this constituency in the House of Commons in Ottawa.

TRANS-CONTINENTAL PEDESTRIANS, 1906

Left to right: G. W. Cumming, John Hugh Gillis, John MacDonald.

In early January of 1906, a North Sydney businessman offered a prize of twelve hundred dollars (twenty-four thousand dollars today) to the first person to walk from North Sydney to the west coast of Canada. These three friends took up the challenge and set out on January 31. Their plan was to follow the railroad tracks from North Sydney to Vancouver and continue on to San Francisco. Cumming and MacDonald dropped out in Montreal, but John Hugh Gillis, my second cousin, continued on to Vancouver, arriving seven months later on September 24. He later became a member of the Vancouver police force.

Standing six feet and four inches tall, John Hugh Gillis was an outstanding athlete who excelled at many sports. In 1911 he was invited by the Amateur Athletic Union of the United States to take part in a pre-Olympic track and field competition. He won eight out of ten events, including the one-hundred-yard dash, the sixteen-pound shot put, the high jump, and the mile run, but for some reason was only awarded a silver medal. The gold medal went to an American!

John Hugh was then invited to join the Canadian Olympic Team for the 1912 Summer Olympics in Stockholm, Sweden. Tragically, however, he developed tuberculosis and died a short while later, at the young age of twenty-nine.

THREE GOOD FRIENDS, 1944

Joe "Clunk" McEwan, Tom Lamie, and Jack MacPherson relax on a sunny afternoon at a taxi stand on Commercial Street. Joe "Clunk," among other odd jobs, was responsible for keeping the downtown streets neat and tidy. Long before mechanized street sweepers, he could be seen pushing a large wooden cart and using a broom and shovel to remove unsightly debris from the streets and lanes. Tom Lamie retired in 1964, after thirty-seven years with the town's fire department. Jack MacPherson, from Antigonish County, worked for many years at the Western Union Cable Office in town.

John and Rannie Gillis, 1947

Nelson Rice made a habit of taking pictures of the neighbourhood children, always outdoors and always with natural light. Enlargements, at no charge, would then be delivered to the surprised and happy parents. I was five and John was three in this photo.

Bibliography

Jackson, Elva. *Cape Breton and the Jackson Kith and Kin*. Windsor: Lancelot Press, 1971.

————————. *Windows on the Past*. Windsor: Lancelot Press, 1974.

Image Sources

Andrea, Marty (Branch 19, Royal Canadian Legion): 88

Beaton Institute, Cape Breton University:
vii, 1, 2, 17, 27, 39, 43-45, 55, 57, 66, 67, 69, 70, 71, 73, 75, 79, 100, 101, 110, 138

Cogan, Jim: 14

Gallivan, Gary:
title page, 8-10, 83, 98, 102, 116

Gillis family:
42, 89, 90, 94, 120, 140

Jesty, Stan:
31, 32

MacDonald, Arlene:
95, 109, 123

McNamara, Frank (St. Joseph's Parish):
93, 96, 97, 99, 103-07, 121

Nelson Rice Collection, Beaton Institute, Cape Breton University:
11, 33, 34, 36, 41, 46, 68, 72, 74, 91, 113 bottom, 124-30, 131, 133-37, 139

North Sydney Historical Society:
ix, xiv, 3-7, 12, 13, 15, 16, 18-26, 28-30, 35, 37, 38, 40, 47, 49-54, 58-63, 65, 76-78, 80-82, 84-87, 92, 108, 111-15, 117-19, 122

Shebib, Robert: 132